# Broke-Free Forever

STRATEGIES TO BREAK FREE FROM
LIVING PAYDAY-TO-PAYDAY.

Be happy & prosperous !

Pam

# Broke-Free Forever

## STRATEGIES TO BREAK FREE FROM LIVING PAYDAY-TO-PAYDAY.

## PAMELA CAREY NELSON, MBA

Carey Management Corp. Kelowna,
British Columbia, Canada

To Daryl, Justin and Darylann

*Life is 10% what happens to you and 90% how you react to it.*

—Charles R. Swindoll

# Contents

# Preface

The thought of money can immediately elicit any one of a wide range of emotions for each of us.

Money can give us opportunities and experiences of profound value; it can save lives, beautify communities, and bring us innumerable comforts and conveniences. Money can also be the source of overwhelming anxiety, anger, and grief. It has been the focal point of countless arguments between otherwise good people. Many of us can testify to the fact that failure to manage our money responsibly leads to general discontent, negativity, and havoc.

And for millions of North Americans, the emotional roller coaster that money represents in our lives is experienced with every single payday—a recurring reminder that we are broke!

But it doesn't have to be that way. In the spring and summer of 2010, twenty-seven households participated in a twelve-week pilot project designed to help them break the cycle of living payday to payday, and *stop being broke*!

Over the twelve weeks, participants worked through the eleven modules included in this book and participated in classroom-type learning workshops to apply what they were learning to their personal financial situation.

At the end of the twelve weeks, participants reported an increased sense of hope for their financial future, less anxiety about personal finances, improved behaviours associated with financial success, decreased negative experiences associated with paydays, and transferable benefits to other areas of their lives. Additionally, participants reported a greater intention and commitment to continue working to achieve personal financial success—two very important factors for achieving change.

*This book was written to help anyone master their personal finances* as quickly as possible, through a simple process of increasing awareness and knowledge and successfully changing behaviour. And, as the many pilot project participants found out, this process works!

Now you too can learn to break the cycle of living payday to payday and live *Broke-Free Forever*. And, you can register online for complimentary (that's free!) access to the downloadable worksheets and spreadsheets, links to online resources, assessments, and tools and sign up for motivational e-coaching to keep you on track!

My intention is to give you access to knowledge, energy, and resources that will help you avoid the payday pain that comes with always feeling "broke." But you might find that while you are focusing on your financial life, other pieces of your life fall into place too.

Be happy; be prosperous.

Pamela Carey Nelson

*Visit BrokeFreeForever.com to access the Book Support website for resources, assessments, e-coaching, and more!*

# Early Praise from Pilot Project Participants:

"I now have the tools, confidence, desire, _goals_, and a compelling reason to succeed in all areas of life. I know that I can create abundance and have financial Freedom in my life. You have the desire to change lives, you will be rewarded. I thank you."
—Ralph W.

"I have a bigger picture now, and know what to do between paycheques. I have a better idea of where I'm going and what I can do to get there." —Raymond W.

"My willingness to take action came from spending time in this program. I have now added to my investments and got back on track. I paid off all my unsecured debt and high interest loans. I read the book cover to cover more than once!" —Janet F.

"The spreadsheets and budget resources I will keep and continue to use in future. There was nothing specific that wasn't relevant, all of the material taught me something new." —Jason H.

"This truly is a great program and[I] truly believe that what you are doing is wonderful work." —Karen G.

# Acknowledgements

Many of my generation grew up in a household where certain things were not spoken of, and that meant we learned about those things through our own, or others', mistakes and successes. My father once told me that "everyone is my superior in some way, and in that, I learn of them." Turns out he was right. As my life took me through many experiences, I became increasingly curious as to what I could learn from others, no matter if it was positive or negative, how I would like to act or not like to act, or created results I would like to emulate or avoid.

Like most "regular" people, my own personal financial experiences have been a roller coaster of ups and downs. I have been broke, and I have been flush. I have learned from both the wisdom and the mistakes of others and my own and have learned much from my professional life and my education. I am honoured to often be asked for my opinion by family, friends, and friends of family.

For years, many of my friends and family have encouraged me to pool my resources together into a book to share with others. Despite how much I love to share my opinion, writing a book is much easier said than done! The final product of this book is a culmination of what I have learned during my own roller-coaster ride and is finally here thanks to the endless encouragement and sometimes even pushy and challenging persistence of those who love me dearly.

After five years, I have finally captured many of my ideas and opinions in this book and have relied on the intelligence and research of many others, as well as my own, to support those ideas. And for that, I have many to thank.

My husband, Daryl, has not only believed in me but has provided the supportive environment to allow me to follow this path. Thank you not only for your love and encouragement, but for the food, shelter, clothing, and personal care.

My son Justin has given me much encouragement. From challenging me to find creative teaching solutions when he was young to giving me some great stories as he matured and grew wiser. My son is my greatest source of pride. Thank you, Justin, for the endless challenges of "*Can you make the spreadsheet do this?*" and for always bringing your friends home believing I could help them, too. Your belief in me as a solutions provider has encouraged my persistence more than you will ever know.

To my stepdaughter Darylann, thank you for allowing me to share my opinions and often unsolicited advice with you! Your presence in my life continues to serve as a source of inspiration to me.

Much acknowledgement goes to all of my (natural, surrogate, and borrowed) nieces, and nephews who allow me to meddle to varying degrees in sorting out their lessons in life—and to share in making fabulous memories as they grow, evolve, and create successes in their own lives. Each of you brings much joy and learning to my life.

When it takes five years to write a book, there are many people who have contributed, whether knowingly or unknowingly. I give a special thank-you to my professional colleagues and friends who have helped answer my questions and direct me to answers and resources and who have contributed in a number of ways towards the finished version of this book and the twelve-week program. Thank you to those who have assisted in the development of this book through contribution, comments, feedback, information, resources, and encouragement: Laurie Mills, Anne-Rachelle McHugh, Lisa Jaffary, Jery Urquhart, Sharleen McBlain, Lara Nemerosky, Sattu Dhaliwal, Laura Gibbs, Anita Bakker, Chelsey Chase, Lydia Ross, Steve Watson, and Patricia Kyle. Finally, thank you to Janet Fidler for helping me find the structure in a mess of information.

Thank you.

# Introduction:
# Payday Pain or Payday Pleasure

**A rich man is nothing but a poor man with money.**
—W. C. Fields

## ■ Lured by Pleasure, Deterred by Pain

Ask yourself these simple questions:

* If you were beginning to feel chilled, would you move out of the shade to the sunny side of a patio?
* Would you relocate your picnic site away from an active wasps' nest?
* Would you get your fingers out of the way when a car door is closing?

If you answered "yes" to the above, congratulations! You're a typical human. Basic behavioural theory suggests all human action is based on either avoiding pain or approaching pleasure.[1] Decisions like those barely enter your conscious thoughts. They are automatic—just simple, common sense, no-brainers! In these situations, our subconscious accesses *knowledge* (including knowledge of painful past experiences) to make automatic decisions and guide our behaviours.

But some of our avoiding-pain decisions are not that automatic. Consider these examples:

* Choosing to wear the eight-second shoes because they look really good
* Procrastinating weeding and feeding the lawn to go play ball or hang out at the lake
* Eating less at dinner so you could enjoy your favourite dessert
* Asking or answering the question, "Do I look fat in this?"
* Going for an early-morning run to make room for the on-the-way-to-work latte

Like these examples, sometimes avoiding pain requires a little more thought. Sometimes we need to contemplate the choices that we have and the implications of the decisions we make. We do that by accessing our knowledge and experiences and using our skills.

That is what this program is about: giving you access to knowledge and skills that will help you modify your behaviours so that sound financial decisions become "no-brainers" in your daily life. My goal is to create automatic responses that bring increased control, satisfaction, and, with time, the pleasure of true financial freedom.

You may have been stung by painful paydays before, but that doesn't mean you need to be stung again! To help you pursue more payday pleasure, *Broke-Free Forever* offers three types of knowledge.

1. Financial—a reevaluation of how money works and how to make simple calculations to help you better analyze your options

2. Self—a clearer understanding of yourself and how your personal relationship with money has evolved thus far

3. Behavioural—knowledge of proven behavioural change factors and processes that can take you step-by-step towards your financial goals

Familiarizing yourself with all three types of knowledge will increase your chances of adjusting your behaviour for making good financial decisions leading to long-term, sustained financial success. Applying this knowledge routinely will help you make good decisions about money automatically. Before too long, you will be able to look back at where you were (are today) and consider just how successful you have become.

## Payday Pain or Payday Pleasure: Two Scenarios

Janice and Sandy are two employees at ABC Manufacturing Co. They do the same job and earn the same salary. Today is payday at ABC, and Janice and Sandy are checking out their pay statements.

### Janice

Janice has a knot in her stomach. She knows there is an extra deduction on this paycheque from the advance she took last week.

She remembers how her over-and-above spending to buy the designer jeans for the dinner party a few weeks back left her with barely enough to cover her mortgage and utilities. She had to tap into this paycheque to cover those expenses. With the realization that her paycheque would barely cover her bills coming due, she considers another two weeks of pasta and beans. "This isn't fair! I work hard...I deserve a break once in a while!" Janice laments.

On the other hand, she thinks about her potential new beau, Ken. He was definitely impressed by her designer jeans and had accepted her invitation for dinner tonight. She wanted to impress him with a home-cooked meal but is embarrassed for Ken to see her home. With the kitchen faucet not working and the fence fallen down, he might soon learn that she can't afford to fix up her fixer-upper! *Screw it,* she thinks. "I'll make a reservation at Gaston's and use the plastic. I'll get caught up next payday," she mutters. Janice picks up the phone and makes a reservation. This evening will totally impress him!

At home, Janice looks through her mail. When she opens her credit card statement, she notices that it's marked overdue. She glances at the interest penalty of $67.90 before considering the minimum monthly payment of $72.00. She's shocked at the amount. It's doubled since last month. She looks at the clock, throws the bill in the drawer, and heads to the shower, whistling. She can't wait to see Ken!

The evening starts well but ends badly. The prices at the restaurant were exorbitant! With the bottle of award-winning wine added to the tab, Janice starts calculating her share. She tries to be sweet and amusing, but her thoughts keep returning to her worsening financial situation. She is wondering just how she will make ends meet when Ken's voice interrupts her thoughts.

"There's a group of us going to the concert in Toronto next month; we're going to make a weekend of it. Do you want to join us?" Of course Janice wants to go! But there is no way she could afford the cost of a ticket, a hotel room, and travel to the concert. She doesn't want to share her financial situation with Ken; she's too embarrassed! They part ways at the end of the evening, and Janice tells Ken she will think about the trip. You never know; she might have room on one of her credit cards.

## Sandy

Sandy opens her pay envelope and immediately casts her glance to the *cumulative RRSP contribution* line item. The total balance is climbing much faster than she had anticipated because her regular contributions are being matched by her employer. Sandy knows that she is building a solid future. She looks forward to the day when she will buy her first home and have a little more spending money at her disposal. She knows she is on a solid path to financial freedom.

A quick calculation indicates she can enjoy a nice date night with Carl on Saturday; after all, the bills are paid. She has enough room in the budget for a couple of steaks for the barbeque, followed by a walk on the seawall, and maybe a rented movie. Six months ago, she was struggling to keep up with the bills and didn't have any plans for her financial future. Back then, she rarely had enough to get through to the next payday.

Sandy isn't making any more money now, but with the effort she's put into managing her finances, she is now in control and headed for a brighter future.

Sandy opens her credit card statement. With regular payments, she has paid off one credit card and can now focus on this, her final outstanding debt. With a balance of $4,200, she figures it will take a few years to pay this one off if she dedicates $150 per month, the total of what she had been paying to the two cards combined. It's a milestone of sorts. Sandy smiles to herself with satisfaction. She can't wait to celebrate with Carl and find out how he has progressed as well. By choosing to share their journey in getting their financial house in order, they are also working towards sharing their home one day.

## What's going on here?

It's hard not to feel sorry for poor (fictitious) Janice. Not only is her love life on shaky ground, but she is in over her head financially.

By splurging on dinner, Janice found a way to experience some pleasure in her otherwise painful payday. But, in doing so, she set herself up for greater pain in the future. She tells herself she has "room" on her MasterCard, but the truth is, by increasing rather than decreasing her debt load, she ends up paying a high interest rate on a balance that will unfortunately just keep getting bigger, whether she makes new purchases or not. Next month, when the costs of the dinner and the old and new interest charges are added to her statement, the minimum monthly payment will probably exceed her ability to pay. She will no longer be able to buy things with the card. To make matters worse, because Janice spends more money than she has available, the money she hasn't even earned yet already belongs to the credit card company.

Sandy, on the other hand, has learned something. In the past, she overspent and lived beyond her means, just like Janice, to the point of accumulating $4,200 in unsecured debt. But, by taking time out to consider her own financial situation, taking control of her spending, and enlisting Carl's support for her change process, Sandy has begun to feel better about her life. She is enjoying herself now and looks forward to even more pleasure in the future.

## A quick number crunch:

If Sandy keeps her credit card off-limits and makes payments of $150 per month, she will have her debt paid off in thirty-eight months (just over three years). Those thirty-eight payments will total $5,700; Sandy will have paid $1,500 in interest (at 19.4 percent) in addition to paying back the $4,200 principal borrowed on that card. (Learn how to do this calculation in the "Psssst! Wanna Buy a Loan?" module). So although Sandy is on the right track, she still has to keep her spending in check for awhile.

Sandy's Situation Recap:

| | |
|---|---|
| 38 payments of | $150 |
| Total debt paid | $5,700 |
| Total interest paid | $1,500 |

At the same interest rate, Janice's $72.00 payment is applied first to the interest fee and then to the principal. At this rate, it will take Janice 179 months (*that's 14.9 years*) to pay off the $4,200 owing. At that rate, Janice will have paid back a total of $12,888.00 (179 payments of $72.00); she will have paid $8,688.00 in interest in addition to paying back the $4,200 principal borrowed with that credit card. *Ouch!* Short-term gain = long-term pain.

Janice's Situation Recap:

| | |
|---|---|
| 179 payments of | $72 |
| Total debt paid | $12,880 |
| Total interest paid | $8,688 |

Sandy is in better financial shape than Janice even though they make the same wage and owe the same amount on their credit cards. The difference between the two is applied knowledge and intention. Sandy knows how her decisions affect her financial future, and Janice doesn't—or doesn't care. Another difference is the focus of their thinking. Sandy improved her financial position by focusing on long-term gain and future success, while Janice's situation worsened because she focused only on short-term gain and immediate success. Because Sandy had long-term goals in mind, she was better able to control her short-term behaviours.

**Your own transition from payday pain to payday pleasure** (and living broke-free forever) may involve a discovery or rediscovery of some of your core values and hidden strengths. It can be an invigorating and rewarding process—one that leads to lasting personal satisfaction and significantly more spending money.

If you are feeling too familiar with Janice's situation, don't despair. You are in good company. Many well-meaning, intelligent, and good-hearted people have been caught in the payday trap. Whether you arrived here as a result of difficult circumstances, lack of information, or good old-fashioned human weakness, recognize that you're not the only one.

All you need to do is use knowledge to gain control of your finances and your behaviour. And a key factor to changing your behaviour is the *desire and intention* to do so.

## ■ Prosperity Versus Money

The focus of *Broke-Free Forever* is to break the cycle of living payday to payday and being broke in between paydays and increase your positive experiences with money. The hard part is to not let money become the central focus your life. That's right: *not* let it become the central focus. The thing is, as much as we'd like to believe that money makes us happier, that's not always true. Having an abundance of money can come with its own set of challenges and is not necessarily the foundation of prosperity. Consider this Belgian Chocolate experience.

### Belgian Chocolate

Researchers studied the relationship between wealth and happiness.[2] They found those people who have more wealth, or were even just thinking about money, had a lower ability to "savour" the finer things in life, such as joy, awe, excitement, pride, and gratitude. When tested to see how they might enjoy eating chocolate, the people who were thinking about money, or even just had more money, felt less enjoyment and even ate their chocolate 30 percent faster!

It is important to put money into perspective in our lives so that the worry and anxiety that might come with having more does not interfere with our ability to enjoy the simple pleasures in life: personal prosperity. So, as you quest for a comfortable life and an abundance of money, don't forget to appreciate the simple pleasures, and savour your chocolate!

# Module 1:
# Show Me Your Marshmallows

*Too many people spend money they haven't earned, to buy things they don't want, to impress people they don't like.*

—Will Rogers

## ■ Peeking Behind the Curtain

It wasn't long ago that people based their spending decisions on three factors: their need for an item, their ability to pay for it, and the value or usefulness of that item. Today, a cultural climate of instant gratification, easy access to credit, and an almost insatiable desire to "keep up with the Joneses" (a.k.a. "affluenza") has many of us spending with little thought as to whether we really want, need, or can pay for the things we buy.

The question is no longer, "Can I afford this?" but "How will this purchase make me look or feel *right now*?" So what has changed? Part of the problem lies in our financial environment in which we have faced increasingly available funds from high-interest and alternative lenders. But a bigger part of the problem is internal—the problem of poorly developed self-control: our inability to self-regulate our own behaviour long enough to bring about the changes we desire and our inability to say no or not now to ourselves.

Delaying gratification comes more naturally to some than others. A study—known today as the marshmallow experiment—provides interesting insight into the issue of self-control and its influence on future success. The study, conducted by Walter Mischel[3] in the late 1960s, tested a group of four-year-olds to see how many could delay eating a marshmallow that had been put in front of them, if it meant they would get two marshmallows just fifteen minutes later.

Results were mixed. Some kids ate the marshmallow immediately while others waited. But what seemed meaningful to Mischel and the other researchers as they followed the children into adolescence and adulthood was that the children who waited were better adjusted, more dependable, and scored higher on aptitude tests. Those who gave in and ate the marshmallow immediately were more likely to have behavioural problems, lower test scores, and difficulty maintaining friendships. As adults, those same kids were less dependable and more likely to have problems with addictive behaviours.

Mischel concluded that self-control is a better indicator of future success than intelligence because it allows people to regulate their behaviours (for example spending) in order to make themselves more successful in the long run.

Does that mean every impulsive child is doomed to a life of self-indulgence and self-sabotage? The answer, thankfully, is no. Mischel's examination of the study in the late 1990s suggests it was the coping mechanisms used by the children with self-control that provided the ability to avoid stressors later in life.[4] Instead of obsessing about the marshmallow and how good it would taste, the patient children in Mischel's study distracted themselves by singing, covering their eyes, or pretending to play hide-and-seek. In short, they controlled their actions by first controlling their thinking.

*View a video example of the marshmallow experiment at BrokeFreeForever.com.*

People who have higher degrees of self-control tend to have better relationships, fewer psychological and emotional symptoms, and higher self-esteem.[5] In short, they are healthier, happier, and more successful. They also tend to have better coping skills, be less aggressive, and do better in school. They are less likely to make impulsive purchases or rash financial decisions.

The good news is that regardless of how little or how much self-control you have practiced in the past, a simple commitment and the right tools are all you need to gain control of your financial future. Regardless of where you are now, it is completely possible to change your behaviour—once you have the facts. Knowledge, commitment, intention, and action can transform all aspects of your financial life, bringing a massive positive impact to your emotional outlook, your career, your professional relationships, and even your love life.

## Show Me Your Marshmallows

Taking control *begins* with honestly recognizing how you have managed your money up until now. Take this self-test to consider your past and present typical money behaviours; your "marshmallows."

This survey is designed to help you look at past behaviours, so the idea is not to pick the "correct answer" or choose the behaviours you know you "should have" or "wish you had" done. Circle the answer that most closely matches your typical past responses to these (or similar) situations.

1.  You have just received a settlement from the insurance company for injuries sustained in a car accident almost two years ago. You have recovered from those injuries and have been feeling great. The settlement is for $21,500. What do you want to do with the money?

    a.  You buy a three-month guaranteed income certificate (GIC) and then spend the next three months researching investment opportunities to determine how you can maximize the greatest return on your investment.

    b.  You make a list of all of your current debts and the associated interest rates and compare that to your wish list of things you want (house, vacation, car, etc.). You spend some time considering how you might make the most of this windfall by paying off some debt and buying something you would not otherwise be able to buy.

    c. Whoo-hoo! It's vacation time! You count out how many vacation days are owing to you at work and search for an exotic and extravagant vacation, like an African safari or European cruise. Of course, you'll need some new shorts and footwear for the trip!

    d. Put it all into your bank account; it'll be gone soon anyhow. Easy come, easy go.

2. You have been invited to attend a going-away party for a friend. This party is going to be held at a very fancy restaurant, and you know the cost is going to be significant. How do you plan for this party?

    a. You send your regrets. You can't afford to spend money recklessly on a night out. Instead, you will send your friend a card and offer to take him/her for coffee on another day.

    b. You plan to attend but will eat dinner beforehand and order a small salad or side plate and a beverage. You start cutting back on other spending and put your savings into an envelope so you will have cash for the event. You will exercise discipline at the restaurant and reward your good behaviour with a treat when you get home.

    c. You start shopping right away for a new outfit so you will be sure to "fit in" to this upscale environment. You can't wait to try the king crab and the award-winning wines you have heard so much about. Oh yes, you will also need a present for your friend.

    d. Of course you'll attend. You put it onto your calendar and will show up when the time comes. If you don't have any money in your bank account, you'll use a credit card. Whatever.

3. You receive your bank statement in the mail (or via e-mail).

    a. You sit down with a pen and compare every item to your own records, making note of any discrepancies so you can call the bank right away.

    b. You review the statement and look up any withdrawals that you don't remember to ensure all is correct and the items make sense.

    c. You look at the balance to see how much money you have. If it's positive, that means you can go out for lunch! If it's negative, you look at how much money is available in your overdraft.

    d. You file it.

4. Your friends are planning a trip to the mountains next weekend and want you to join them. You haven't planned for this trip and have a number of bills due before next payday.

    a. You decline, but thank them for the offer. You did not budget for this frivolous trip.

    b. You calculate how much money you have left over after all your bills are paid and then call your friends to find out how you might share expenses to make the trip affordable. You will go only if you can keep the expenses within the limits of what you can afford.

    c. Sweet. You start packing.

    d. Sounds like fun. You tell your friend you'd be happy to catch a ride with them because your gas tank is low, and you will sleep on the couch so you don't have to worry about the cost of a room.

5. Your television "kicks the bucket," and you don't have a second one. One of your credit cards is maxed out, but you have another one.

    a. You let all your friends know that you need a TV and would be happy to take an old one off their hands should they have one kicking around. Failing that, you visit the secondhand store to see what you can find.

    b. You plan to put some money away for the next few paydays and start reviewing flyers to find the best deal. The more cash you can save, the less debt you will have to incur.

    c. Now you can go and buy the big-screen HDTV you've been wanting. After all, there are no payments or interest for six months. You survey your friends to find out what they have so you can get one that's bigger and better.

d. Oh well. You've got a bunch of books you've been meaning to read and lots of downloaded movies on your computer.

6. You receive a final notice for your cell phone warning you that service will be discontinued in two weeks if full payment isn't made. The final notice includes an interest penalty of $126.

a. You immediately pull the file that contains all of your past bills and payment receipts. The phone company has obviously made a mistake because you know you pay your bill on the same date every month. You have all of the evidence you need to make sure they correct this right away.

b. You review your last few months' bills to calculate what you have paid. You know you have been making payments on the balance owing and can't imagine what is going on. You will call them to find out why they haven't received your payments.

c. Oh crap. You meant to pay it later but completely forgot. You will pay the outstanding balance—but not the interest; that's just not fair!

d. That's strange; you don't remember receiving any bills from them since you moved three months ago. How dare they threaten to cut off your service when you haven't even received a bill from them! It's not your fault if they can't get your address right! They can't possibly expect you to pay some random amount without knowing how they came up with that number!

7. Your work colleague shares how she and her husband met with a financial planner and worked out a plan to help them reach their retirement goals.

a. You ask her who they met with. You will call to make an appointment yourself. It's never too late to start planning!

b. You ask her what it cost. No doubt a financial planner will cost big bucks—everyone seems to want a piece of the action these days!

c. Planning shmanning—whatever!

d. You'll worry about that when you need to. Right now, there are other more important things to focus on. Retirement is so far away, and you're certain that the government isn't going to let you starve.

Now, review your answers and consider how satisfied you are with your responses. Do you think your current behaviour will lead you to serious trouble? Is it okay, but there is room for improvement? Or is your behaviour on track for a successful financial future and couldn't be better?

## ■ Why Do We Do the Things We Do?

Albert Einstein said it best in his definition of insanity: "Doing the same thing over and over and expecting different results."

If you have been unhappy with the results of your past financial management, you will probably want to consider changing your behaviour to get different results. For most of us, simply recognizing the difference between payday pain and payday pleasure gives us the incentive we need to take action. But, before we talk about *how* to change our sometimes self-sabotaging behaviours, let's take a step back and consider what may be behind some of those behaviours.

Our "one-marshmallow" money behaviours can be traced to a variety of sources, including our personal beliefs, our attitudes, and our personalities, as well as the circumstances and pressures that we face in our individual lives. The following sections look at these sources in order to help identify some factors that may contribute to how we manage our money.

⌘ ⌘ ⌘

### *True Story: Gonna Die Broke*

I once had a friend who believed he was going to "die broke" and was well on his way to achieving that self-fulfilling prophecy. It turns out that as a child, he had worked very hard with two paper routes to earn and save his money. But there was an adult in his life who found that burgeoning piggy bank a handy nickel-and-dime loans department. No matter how hard John worked to save his money, this adult's frequent "borrowings" and empty promises to repay rendered the piggy bank empty. Finally, John quit his newspaper job and quit trying to get ahead.

Decades later, in his fifties, John had a zero net worth. John wasn't a stupid man, but he was trapped in a cycle. He frequently entered into high-interest loans or bad deals. Whenever he saved up some money, he would blow it on something unimportant or lose it in a bad deal. Because of these self-sabotaging behaviours, he had no retirement fund or savings. Now he was starting to worry about how he would support himself as he aged. Could he still change his fate?

Difficult early experiences sometimes leave us with little faith in the future. You may have trouble envisioning and embracing future rewards if you find it hard to believe that the second marshmallow actually exists. Sometimes, just recognizing the root of this issue is all it takes to gain freedom. If issues are deeply rooted, it may be wise to seek professional counsel.

⌘ ⌘ ⌘

## Beliefs

We each hold many beliefs about ourselves, others, places, things, and ideas. Some of these beliefs we are aware of, and some of them are lingering in the background of our actions without much thought or awareness. Our beliefs guide our interpretations of reality.

Henry Ford was convinced that everything in a person's life is the way it is, because he or she wants it that way. "Whether you think you can or whether you think you can't, you're right!" Ford once said. Ford and many others believed that we create the life we want. Every day, people everywhere draw conclusions, make decisions and choices, and converse based on their inventory of positive and negative beliefs about themselves and the world around them. It's true that beliefs can be very powerful, and we can hold on to them with great conviction.

Just as our beliefs influence our perceptions, beliefs also drive our behaviour. But, strangely enough, many of our beliefs are *not* based on experience; in fact, they *rarely* are. Our beliefs can, and often do, override the evidence of our experiences, a phenomenon that can work to our advantage or disadvantage. False beliefs can be counterproductive when we are trying to gain or integrate real knowledge. Socrates once stated, "The unexamined life is not worth living." Perhaps then some of our unexamined beliefs may not be worth holding on to either.

Beliefs can be difficult to identify. Sometimes, understanding what you actually believe (even if it's not productive) helps you to move towards the beliefs you would like to embrace. Consider the following statements to identify some of your own beliefs, and what beliefs you might have based on past experiences but may not necessarily hold true under scrutiny, today.

1. Successful people create their own luck: luck is what happens when preparation meets opportunity.

2. I am responsible to shape my own destiny. I not only have the right, but the responsibility to work to achieve my potential.

3. Asking for help or advice is a sign of strength. Acknowledging someone else's expertise or skill does not diminish my own value.

4. I deserve and am worthy of financial success. Why not me?

5. Overcoming obstacles will ultimately help me grow and become stronger.

6. Having money will enable me to do more. Money is not the root of all evil; it provides the ability to be generous!

7. There is no relationship between money and integrity; you can have one without the other.

8. When I think about reducing my expenses and being frugal to get ahead financially, I feel powerful and have great hope for my future.

## Changing Your Beliefs

If you are holding on to beliefs that are not serving you in your quest for personal financial success, don't despair. Changing belief systems is the subject of much research and practical application.

Studies show you first need to un-confirm the old thoughts and beliefs.[6] You need to understand why they no longer fit and acknowledge that fact. The less your old beliefs make sense, the easier they are to get rid of. Disempowering old beliefs will help you make room in your mind for new beliefs. Each time you find yourself thinking the "old" thought or belief, catch yourself and say, "No" (and you can use your inside or your outside voice!). Then replace that belief by saying, "Yes," to a new one.

To create a new belief you have to say, "Yes," to it repeatedly. Frequency and emotional intensity are required to cement the relationship between action and outcome in your mind. The process of proving the new belief *to yourself* creates the proof you need. Your mind will take it from there.

## Who's in control here anyway?

When people consider the concept of personal destiny, their beliefs tend to lean in one of two directions: an internal or external locus of control. Those who operate from an external locus of control believe they are at the mercy of fate, luck, or chance or that the outcomes of their lives are dictated by other people.

Research conducted on five continents suggests that people who believe they control the outcomes of their lives (those exercising an internal locus of control) are generally more motivated and achievement orientated.[7] The research suggests "internals" tend to take more responsibility and achieve better results in their personal and professional lives. Luckily, locus of control is a perception, not a hardwired personality trait. Perceptions can be changed.

*Take the online Locus of Control assessment at BrokeFreeForever.com.*

## Do you have a "rescue" fantasy?

Many of us grew up believing in fairy tales and superheroes; we loved stories about damsels being rescued by knights in shining armour or Batman saving the entire city. These images are connected to the belief that bad things really won't happen to good people or when bad things do happen, someone (or something) will come to the rescue.

While heroism and altruism are not to be discounted, a fantasy of rescue could prevent you from taking action to improve your own situation. For some people, the belief that an inheritance, a lottery win, a wealthy suitor, God, the government, or their family will step in and reverse the results of poor financial management takes away the sense of urgency and responsibility to provide for their own future.

If you are fortunate enough to have a fairy godmother or other safety net, that's a good thing, but take a moment to consider your belief (it may be disguised as hope!) in rescue may actually be preventing you from taking responsibility for your own situation. And do remember that any safety net is subject to its own set of realities.

* Lottery/Gambling—Yes, you could win, but you could also lose. Everybody pays to play the odds.

* Government—Governments change every few years, so do economic circumstances and policies.

* White knights—Sighhhh. Seems they're a threatened population.

* Counting on an inheritance? Your luck may also be constrained by competition (number of cousins) and resources; maybe Uncle Joe's entire estate is only worth $5,000. Keep in mind that many estates dwindle rapidly when the benefactor has medical costs to pay.

Our greatest superhero is ourselves.

## Values

Our values are those principles that shape our choices. They are those underlying principles of importance that bring meaning to our life, those things we hold dear and treasure. We can value an attitude, a belief, a personality trait, a situation, a condition, a way of being—there are few rules around values.

Our values can be closely related to our beliefs, and they definitely impact our behaviour and decisions.

We don't often give much thought to our values, that is, until someone questions them or something threatens them. Our values can (and do!) change over time, and our prioritization of our values will change depending on our current pressures and internal and external factors.

Let's check in and consider those values that are important to us now with the following exercise. Review the following list of values. Choose between twelve to fifteen that resonate with you currently.

| | | |
|---|---|---|
| adventure | sassiness | kindness |
| excitement | commitment | supportiveness |
| power, control | gutsiness | co-operation |
| authenticity | security | laughter |
| fairness | communications | trustworthiness |
| recognition | health | creativity |
| balance | sexuality | learning |
| family | community | understanding |
| relaxation | helping others | discipline |
| boldness | sharing | loyalty |
| fitness | competence | vanity |
| respect | honesty | diversity |
| bravery | solitude | mindfulness |
| freedom | competition | variety |
| responsibility | hope | education |
| clarity | spirituality | objectivity |
| friendship | confidence | wealth |
| risk taking | independence | environment |
| cleanliness | spontaneity | physical challenge |
| generosity | confidentiality | working hard |
| safety | intellectual challenge | equality |
| cohesiveness | structure | play and fun |
| graciousness | consideration | worthiness |

Next, review your selections, pick a maximum of eight as being the most important to you. Don't worry if you *think* something should be on your list that doesn't make the final cut. The idea is to identify those few that are of top priority to you currently. It is guaranteed that some things you hold important may not make it to the top eight—and that's okay! It doesn't make them unimportant, just less so at this time.

Now arrange those eight in order of priority, from the most important to least important. Which values are in your top three at the present time?

Now consider: How might these values be affecting your behaviour and decisions in the present?

Considering your financial past, what values might have helped shape where you are today?

## Got 'Tude?

It seems that some people are generally cheerful and all sunshiny all the time, while others can find something wrong with any situation. Your attitude is your general feeling towards something. Your attitude reflects how much you like or dislike something and whether you feel positively or negatively about something. And yes, your attitude affects your money behaviour.

It is widely accepted in our society that we all get to choose our attitude; it is completely within our control. Use the following to check in and rate your own money attitude. Check how closely each of the following statements describes your attitude towards your personal finances.

### What is your money attitude?

Consider each of the statements below, and place a check mark next to those that match your own money attitude.

__ I love shopping; it makes me feel better (retail therapy).

__ Eating eat out is too expensive! I take the time to make my own lunch to bring to work.

__ I like to acquire. Whoever has the biggest TV or the most toys (or the most pairs of shoes) wins.

__ Credit is a useful tool to help me "fit in" and belong.

__ I gotta live for today; I want to enjoy life while I can. Who cares if I have to pay for it over the next year?

__ Saving is very important. I save and pay cash for everything, including essentials.

__ My financial planner helps me to keep my future in mind. Every decision I make today impacts my tomorrow.

__ Everyone uses credit; it's no big deal. I couldn't make ends meet without it.

__ Just because I have credit doesn't mean I have to use it. My credit cards are for emergencies only.

__ A penny saved is a penny earned! I always use coupons.

__ Having security is responsible. I feel secure knowing I have three to six months of expenses saved.

__ I *hate* paying bills! Sometimes I don't open them on time-and miss the payment due date.

__ I don't like owing anybody anything. I pay every bill as soon as it arrives.

__ I don't like having to read contracts and fine print; who cares about that stuff anyway?

__ I like to know the total cost of any financial decision before I commit. I will take the time to consider before making a decision.

__ Everyone is out to take my money from me. You can't get blood from a rock!

Now, review your answers. Were you truthful? Review the attitudes you've identified and consider whether you were accurate in your assessment or whether you answered how you think your attitude *should* be. Adjust any of your answers if necessary for accuracy. Then, work through the list again identifying the statement(s) that you would like to change. Circle, mark, or highlight them for future consideration. This information will be useful during the goal-setting module.

### Emotional Spending

Have you ever stopped to think about *why* you spend money on things? Most people don't. But it might be worth the effort!

Here are some thoughts on that subject; so see if any of these hit home for you.

### Power

I'm not talking about the kind of power that makes your lights work; I mean relationship power. A balance or imbalance of power exists in every relationship—to some extent. Power is the ability one has to influence another's behaviour.[8]

See if you can identify the type of power the relationships in the following example might have. Put the letter that corresponds to the *type of power* next to the name or description in the second column (answers below*):

| | |
|---|---|
| a) Legitimate (recognized authority ) | _____ Oprah or Simon Cowell |
| b) Expert (based on knowledge or skill) | _____ Security Guard or Police |
| c) Referent (based on notoriety or popularity) | _____ Plumber or Accountant |
| d) Coercive (using threat or force) | _____ Supervisor, Employer |
| e) Reward (ability to compensate as desired) | _____ Parent, Guardian |

Research has shown that individuals who feel powerless are willing to pay higher prices for something that makes them feel more powerful.[9] While they may gain an increased (but false) sense of restored power in their lives, they are also more likely to overspend and sink into a deepening pit of debt. This can quickly become a losing cycle of spending, feeling a lack of power, spending more, feeling overwhelmed by debt (and powerless), spending more to recapture it...you get the drift.

### Status

I previously made reference to wanting to "keep up with the Joneses." Well, I don't know about the Joneses, but you might be driven to spend to impress your colleagues, family, or friends (though I would definitely question how good of friends you have, if you feel you must always impress them!).

---

* Answers: Oprah or Simon Cowell—c; security guard or police—d; plumber or accountant—b; supervisor or employer—e (could arguably also be a); parent or guardian—a (could arguably also be e).

Even if you are feeling all powerful and in control of your life, you might be motivated to buy that new motorbike, big-screen television, or new dining room suite because your friend, sister, brother-in-law, or co-worker has one. If you feel tempted to buy "a status item," take some time, step back from the cash register, and consider what's motivating the purchase. Put it aside for at least a week. Oh yes, check out the "Dream / Delay / Design" exercise in the "Frugal—the *Good* F-word" section of Module 4.

### Rosy Outlook

*Things are going great, and they're only getting better*
*I'm doing all right, getting good grades*
*The future's so bright, I gotta wear shades.*

Within these lyrics, Pat McDonald [10] captures that feeling we have all experienced at some point. There are those days when you feel like you're on top of the world. Everything is going well; your cares are few and far between. The birds are singing; the sun is warming your face...ahhhhh, what a wonderful feeling!

But look out! Though we strive to achieve that wonderful, optimistic, rosy outlook, it can be a feeling that gets us into trouble financially! Why? Because a rosy outlook encourages us to spend money.

Have you ever made a purchase, large or small, in anticipation of a good day, a raise, a windfall, or some other wonderful something to celebrate? If you think long enough, I'm certain you will come up with an example. When we believe that our "future looks bright," we tend to believe we deserve a treat. When our financial pressure is about to be eased, we believe that the purchase will not have a negative effect. In other words, when *something* positive is *expected* to happen, we tend to be less cautious in our spending.

## Guilt

More powerful than a locomotive, guilt can bring a grown-up to his/her knees. And, right or wrong, it is one of the most powerful mobilisers (or demobilisers) known to humankind.

Guilt is widely considered to be an emotion that helps us regulate our behaviour. Guilt is a feeling of remorse (sadness) that tends to motivate us into one of two actions: either avoidance or restitution and amends.

Guilt is most likely to affect our spending habits when we want to make amends. A parent returning from a business trip might buy a high-priced gift for her child at the airport gift shop (ever wonder why there are so many stores in an airport?). A financially strapped husband might use a credit card to purchase an expensive piece of jewellery to make up for forgetting his wedding anniversary.

Spending beyond your means is not the wisest option for assuaging your guilty feelings. If you are motivated to spend money on something because you are feeling guilty, take a few moments to consider why you are feeling guilty and what other options you have to make amends.

## *I'm Just Saying*

Guilt and worry are two nonproductive emotions. We tend to worry about something that *might* happen in the future; we feel guilty about something that *has happened* in the past.

If you are concerned about something that could happen in the future (worry), you have the opportunity to take action to alleviate whatever outcome you fear. So don't worry; do something about it—whatever "it" may be!

If you are feeling remorseful about something that has happened in the past (guilt), you can't do anything to change it—the past is history—but you may be able to make amends, relieve the feelings of remorse, and restore a relationship. So, do something about it—within your budget. When you "do something about it," you are taking control—of yourself, your actions, and your life. Be responsible, be accountable, and take action.

## Money Can't Buy Me Love

Despite the efforts of many marketers to make you believe otherwise, money cannot buy love. It can buy groceries; it can buy shelter; it can buy gifts; it can buy *things* and *experiences*…but money cannot buy love.

If you find yourself buying gifts for someone as an expression of your love, you may need to examine whether you are motivated by guilt. While the gift may bring a smile to the face of the person receiving it, it may not speak "love" to him or her.

In his book *The Five Love Languages*, Gary Chapman presents the idea that just as each of us has a predominant personality or communication style, we also have a predominant "love language."[11] Chapman describes the five languages as words of affirmation, quality time, receiving gifts, acts of service and physical touch. If you truly want to express your heartfelt love for someone, first identify that person's primary love language, and then use that language to show your love instead of automatically using money or gifts.

## Soft Touch

We frequently refer to people who give in easily to others or who have trouble standing up for themselves as "not having a backbone." Another popular reference is "soft touch." Either way, people who tend to be constantly taken advantage of because they have difficulty saying, "No," can find themselves spending more money, or even lending money to others, when they can't really afford to.

If you find yourself lending money to others or paying for things when you know you shouldn't, think about why you are having trouble saying, "No." Others can take advantage of you only when you let them. If need be, enlist the aid of a trusted family member, counsellor, clergyperson, teacher, community resource centre, or professional whom you trust to help you find alternatives to being powerless.

## Disconnection

Our minds are pretty powerful weapons. When we don't want to face the truth, it is very easy for us to disconnect and deny the reality of our own situation.

A great example of disconnecting is in the use of credit cards. When we use a credit card to pay for something, we don't experience the value of that money leaving our wallets or bank accounts, and this leads to a state of disconnection with *the reality* of how much money we now have, or now owe. (Owe is Ow spelt with an "e.") Because you do not *feel* or *see* the money leaving your possession, you may not fully comprehend the amounts of money you are spending. Sometimes credit can seem like an endless resource—a money tree—until we receive the bill. Even then, it is easy to forget that painful "amount due" between statement dates. Every time you use credit, you are spending money that you haven't made yet, even if you pay the card off each month.

### Because You're, Well, Um, Perhaps a Wee Bit Lazy?

Let's call a spade a spade. Sometimes people spend because they are too lazy not to. Stopping to buy a pizza or pick up fast foods on the way home from work takes much less effort than making a meal at the end of the day or planning in the morning by using your slow-cooker, especially if you are tired.

Buying that juicy-sounding paperback is easier than going to the library to borrow a book. Driving to your workplace every day is much more convenient than taking the bus, walking, or riding a bike. Buying frozen, prepared meals is much more convenient than making a casserole from scratch. The trouble is, convenience comes at a premium price. In addition to saving hundreds over a few months by home-brewing your coffee for the daily commute, you can save additional hundreds by making meals from scratch. How much do you spend every week or month on gas and parking to get to work? How much would you save if you took the bus, rode your bike, or walked? Use the exercise below to find out.

**Automobile Cruncher Exercise:** Determine how much your ride really costs you.

Monthly Cost

How much do you pay for insurance?
Divide your annual cost by 12 months, or insert your
monthly payment.

_____

How much do you pay for gas?
Multiply your average weekly cost by 52 and then
divide by 12, or insert your monthly average.

_____

How much do you pay for repairs and
maintenance over a one year period? (Don't
forget to include tires, check-ups and oil changes.)
Estimate your annual costs and then divide by 12,
or insert your monthly average.

_____

**TOTAL all of the above:**
**This is how much your ride costs per month.**   _____

Some questions to ponder:

* How does the true monthly cost compare with alternatives, such as the bus or your bike?

* How much of your monthly income are you spending each month on your ride? (Divide the above total by your monthly income to calculate percent.)

* How many hours of wages do you need to earn to pay your monthly total?

Transportation and food aren't the only examples of premium-priced convenience options, but they are the most common. Take a few moments to think of other convenience choices that you or your family members make where there are other options that could save money.

## Hierarchy of Needs

A well-known theory of human motivation is referred to as Maslow's Hierarchy, aptly named after Abraham Maslow, the researcher/psychologist who studied mentally healthy individuals.

Maslow believed people possess a strong desire to reach a level of full potential: a status of self-actualization.[12]

According to Maslow's hierarchy, every human being has five levels of "needs" that must be substantially satisfied before that person can progress through to the next higher level. Maslow's hierarchy of five needs includes (in order from highest to lowest):

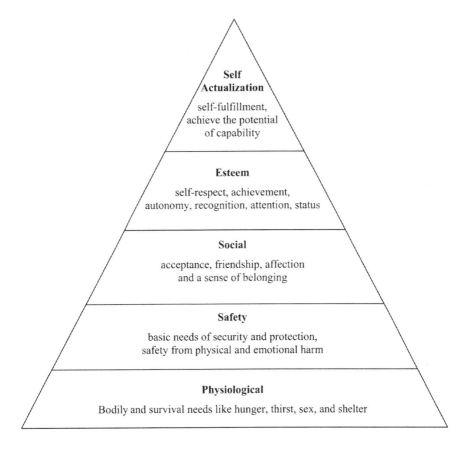

Depending on what level of the hierarchy of needs you are currently operating at, you may be motivated to spend money. Fulfilling basic needs at the physiological and safety levels could include obvious examples like rent and food. At the social level, you might feel motivated to buy presents for friends or host a dinner party; at the esteem level, you may want to upgrade your choice of vehicle; and, at the self-actualization level, you may want go back to school (pay tuition). These are just some examples, of course. How motivational needs come into play in your personal spending and financial choices is as unique as you are!

## Life Stages

There are numerous points on our life timeline that will greatly impact our money behaviours. Some significant timeline points are graduation, job changes, relationship changes, adding children to the mix, preparing for retirement, taking care of elderly parents and supporting our own children through their life changes.

Depending on where you are right now may have greatly influenced your decision to examine your money behaviours. So where are you? Look at the horizontal lifeline below. At the far left is the moment of your birth and the far right is the last day of your life. Where on that line do you consider yourself to be? What past events have affected your money behaviours and what future events do you think may come to pass?

Consider what events those future stages may hold, and how they will affect your money behaviours.

### *Will*power or *Won't*-power?

Self-control allows us to resist temptation and say no to things we'd like to buy, eat, have, drive, etc. It was the subject of the marshmallow experiments we considered previously. Research has determined that self-control is like a muscle. Prolonged exercise of self-control depletes our reserves and weakens our resistance to the temptations we want to avoid.[13] Though muscle strength can be increased over time with exercise, muscle power is limited on a daily basis; muscles will eventually tire under strain, and the activity has to stop. Just like a muscle, when self-control is constantly exerted, its strength is depleted, even though over time, the strength of our ability to control behaviours increases with regular use.

This means we are less likely to expend self-control under strain. It's like holding your breath: you can only do it for so long. Knowing the factors that can sidetrack your self-control will help you practice it more effectively. The research indicates there are certain conditions that will lead to a depletion of self-control:

* **Too many choices**—Being surrounded by an endless array of options will deplete willpower.

* **Timing**—Most people are more able to practice self-control in the early morning. Our willpower reserves are replenished as we sleep, allowing us to be more self-controlled in the morning. In the afternoon or evening, we may be more likely to abdicate self-control.

* **Decisions, decisions!**—People are more vulnerable to temptations and impulsive behaviours at the end of the day after being worn down by the progressive need to make decisions throughout the day. Be on guard on days when you have to make multiple decisions.

* **Stress**—Worry and frustration or pressure from a variety of sources can stimulate impulsive behaviours.

* **Physical conditions**—Physical circumstances can diminish our self-control. We are less likely to act rationally when we feel tired, hungry, or sick, or when under the influence of alcohol or drugs.

* **Regularity of Routines**—Having a regular grocery-buying day and using a list will go a long way towards staying on track. By living our lives on autopilot, we diminish the need for making conscious decisions, a known detriment to our willpower resources.

* **Not Keeping Track**—People tend to lack self-control when they don't monitor their spending. People who successfully quit smoking, lose weight, or train for a long run usually track their progress to provide motivation and help them keep their ultimate goal in sight.

Perhaps Mom was right: making plans, getting enough sleep, staying healthy, and practicing good money management behaviours (like the ones suggested in this book) will help you to exercise and strengthen your self-control.

But beware, being aware of self-control is only half the battle. Temptation is mighty powerful and tests our ability to self-regulate on many levels. It turns out that our confidence in our ability to refrain from giving in to temptation can be a grave downfall.

Recent research suggests that people who had a heightened (inflated) sense of their ability to self-control were most likely to miscalculate how well they could avoid temptation and were more likely to expose themselves to greater degrees of temptation.[14] This ultimately led to their surrender to that temptation. So if you are quite confident that you can avoid temptation, that may be a red flag that you should expend extra effort to avoid temptation in the first place.

# ■ Summary of Module 1

In this module, we have taken a look behind the scenes at some of the factors that may be contributing to our money management behaviours.

Scrutinizing our financial habits and the things that have influenced those habits allows us to start fresh. New insights and awareness will help us to avoid repeating old patterns and create productive new ones.

## Money-Boosting Strategies from Module 1:

Strategy #1:  Know your ability to self-regulate; apply self-discipline.

Strategy #2:  Be aware of your money behaviours, attitudes and beliefs.

Strategy #3:  Understand why you spend your money.

## Access these Module 1 exercises and resources at BrokeFreeForever.com:

Money Behaviours
Personal Beliefs
Locus of Control
My Values
Financial Attitude
Reflection Questions

# Module 2:
## Mirror, Mirror, on the Wall

*It is not only our right, it's our responsibility to work to achieve our potential.*

—Roberta Bondar

## ■ My, what a nice personality you have!

Most of us know that physical attractiveness and personality are not directly related. Our personalities, and our financial management styles, however, may be. That being the case, it might be helpful to look at the various ways your personality connects with your money management so that you can incorporate your strongest personal traits into a recipe for financial success.

### Second Opinion: Laurie Mills, M.Ed., CHRP, CPC, Certified Professional Coach

When we understand our own behaviour patterns we can deal with life's ups and downs in healthier, more effective ways. By better understanding how and why we act as we do, we also get insights into others' behaviour. This is important because our interactions with others—family, friends, spouses, kids, co-workers— greatly impact the choices we make.

One way to accelerate self-awareness is through the use of personality assessments. Any in-depth personality assessment requires a trained professional to administer and interpret it. There are many no-cost or low-cost online versions of personality testing available, but one word of caution: do not take the results from these free tests too literally. They are simply not designed to provide an in-depth analysis of your personality and behaviour. But they do have value because they can get you thinking about your own behaviours and how they might be experienced by others. Since it isn't easy to see yourself objectively, you might use your personality profile reports to do a reality check with the people who know you best or spend the most time with you, like family and work colleagues.

The intent here is not to put yourself out there for criticism but to get honest feedback on how others see you. By getting a few opinions, you may be surprised to find that others see strengths in you that you didn't realize you had.

The whole purpose of using personality assessments is to increase our self-awareness with regard to how we behave and how we interact with others. In that learning, we can build appreciation of our own unique gifts and find ways to work to our strengths more often.

⌘ ⌘ ⌘

A widely accepted personality model is known as the Big Five Model.[15] This model supports that there are five basic dimensions of personality, and all personality traits can be categorized into one of these five dimensions. The Big Five include: extroversion, agreeableness, conscientiousness, emotional stability, and openness to experience. Each are described below.

Using the ten-point scale, how would you self-rate your own personality, generally, on each of the five personality dimensions?

### Extraversion / Introversion

This dimension indicates how one is energized: through the external world or the internal world. Extraverts seek relationships with others and often use the talk-it-out approach to processing their thoughts. Introverts generally want time to think things through and prefer a slower paced conversation. They are unlikely to share personal information with those they do not know well. On a scale of 1 to 10, indicate below how extraverted or introverted you think you are, where 0 indicates an internal preference and 10 indicates an external preference.

## Agreeableness

This dimension indicates how agreeable or cooperative you are with others, how "good-natured" you are, and how trusting of others you may be. Rate how agreeable/cooperative you think you are, where 0 leans towards antagonistic and 10 means you must guard against being someone's doormat.

## Conscientiousness

How reliable, orderly, and dependable are you? A highly conscientious person may be described as thoughtful with goal-directed behaviours and good impulse control. This person tends to be organized and detail oriented. Rate how conscientious you believe yourself to be, where 0 means you are less orderly and more impulsive and 10 means you are more organized and achievement-focused.

## Emotional Stability / Neuroticism

A person who is neurotic worries a lot and is prone to anxiety. They may also suffer from depression, insecurity, and nervousness. An emotionally stable person is typically calm, self-confident, and able to withstand stressful situations. Rate your degree of emotional stability, where 0 indicates anxious, nervous, and insecure and 10 indicates calm and self-confident.

| 1 | 2 | 3 | 4 | 5 | 6 | 7 | 8 | 9 | 10 |

## Openness to Experience

"Open" people tend to have active imaginations and are considered insightful and curious. They tend to have a broad range of interests and a high degree of independence. A person with a lower degree of "openness" might be described as being close-minded and quite comfortable with the familiar. Rate how open to experience you are, where 0 means not at all open and 10 means you are curious, creative, and have an active imagination.

| 1 | 2 | 3 | 4 | 5 | 6 | 7 | 8 | 9 | 10 |

## Relationship to Money

Our personality traits greatly influence our decisions. Some people are naturally inclined to make decisions based on critical thinking and logic, while others may utilize brainstorming, visualization, and clarification of values.[17] Some traits are stronger than others and have an influence in everything that we do (primary), while others tend to be less consistent and even dependent on the situation—they come and go or flex depending on the situation, such as when you are tired, stressed, panicked, or excited (secondary).[18] Once you have determined your own primary and secondary personality traits, you can then examine how those traits influence your money behaviours.

The influence of trait type (Myers-Briggs) and temperament (Keirsey) on financial planning has been explored by a number of researchers. A report on the implications of psychological type on financial behaviour was published by the Association for Financial Counseling and Planning Education in their *Journal of Financial Counseling and Planning*. This report summarized some of the general implications to Myers-Briggs trait types as follows.

### Extravert Versus Introvert

Extraverts may be more ready and willing to speak with financial planners and may change their financial plans with subsequent input. On the other hand, introverts may want to peruse written materials and take the time to read and consider the material before meeting with a planner. Introverts are also more likely to have a "conservative" investment portfolio.

### Sensing Versus Intuitive

These traits describe the process relied on to gather information. Some people are more trusting of their senses and focus on the present and concrete ideas. Intuitive people may use hunches and intuition to process information, prefer brainstorming ideas, and see the "big picture." Sensing people make good comparison shoppers and like to consider examples, whereas intuitives want to think about their future and are more apt to consider creative financial alternatives, such as bartering and sharing.

### Thinking Versus Feeling

This describes how people make decisions. Someone who prefers a logical and scientific approach and likes to consider numbers and figures is more *thinking*, whereas a person with a *feeling* disposition prefers harmony and considers the feelings of others, sometimes to the point of accommodating other's feelings at the expense of their own. Thinking people tend to consider cost-benefit trade-offs and are less emotionally tied to their money and financial plans (highly objective). More feeling people may seek socially conscious–based investments and may not be as vocal in asking questions when they don't understand something.

### Judging Versus Perceiving

This describes one's lifestyle orientation. People with a *Judging* orientation are considered more decisive and orderly; they make plans regularly and are more prone to long-term (retirement) planning. *Perceiving*-oriented people like to keep their options open and may work best when deadlines are approaching. They may not be as eager to keep track of their finances and are not as apt to make systematic plans or implement any plans.

## Your Big Five – A Review

Now let's review the Big Five dimensions. Refer back to your self-assessment of the Big Five traits and consider how they might influence your money behaviours. Alignment of the Myers-Briggs types to each of the Big Five dimensions is included for reference.[19] While the relationships between the dimensions and the types are not necessarily direct, they do lend some commonalities that may be helpful for considering your own styles.

### Extroversion/Introversion *(Extroversion/Introversion)*

People who are lively or outgoing may find themselves in more social situations where the temptation to spend is greater. When it comes to making larger purchase decisions, they may be more influenced by other people's input and experiences.

At the other end of the scale, people who are more introverted may spend more time at home than socializing (which may or may not affect the entertainment budget!) and would probably rely more on their own research for purchase decisions.

How does your degree of extroversion show up in your money behaviours? Record your thoughts.

### Agreeableness *(Feeling/Thinking)*

Highly agreeable people are typically more trusting and may be more willing to spend easily and generously. When it comes to making larger purchase decisions, they might be less cautious and not do their homework as thoroughly, increasing the likelihood of post-purchase regret.

Less agreeable people may be more cynical and scrutinize the fine print more carefully. When it comes to record-keeping, they might be more precise and organized—if for no other reason than to be able to prove others wrong! They might be more cautious with their spending—after all, why would anyone want to give their hard-earned money to someone else?

How does your degree of agreeableness show up in your money behaviours? Record your thoughts.

### *Conscientiousness (Judging / Perceiving)*

If you scored yourself higher on this scale, you may be more apt to pay your bills on time and track your spending to the penny. You might be more comfortable with following a budget and making larger purchase decisions based on how the purchase fits in with your goals, weighing the pros and cons before making any final decision.

Less conscientious people may keep their tax receipts and records in a shoe box (if at all!) and may not know where any of their money goes. Creditors may make oodles of money from you because you end up paying larger amounts of interest on your overdue bills, and your friends may consider any money lent to you as gone forever.

How does your degree of emotional stability show up in your money behaviours? Record your thoughts.

### Emotional Stability

The lower your emotional stability, the greater likelihood that your emotions dictate your spending. You might be too depressed to even think about the long-term impact of today's purchase decisions. Your insecurity may make it difficult to stand up for yourself when being taken advantage of, and you may find making a larger purchase decision a nerve-wracking experience.

If you are emotionally strong, you may be more self-confident and have higher expectations for your investments. You may be a significant contender for any salesperson who works on commission, and you are less apt to panic when economists warn of increasing interest rates and stock-market volatility.

How does your degree of conscientiousness show up in your money behaviours? Record your thoughts.

### Openness to Experience (Intuition/Sensing)

If you have a highly open personality, you may be fascinated with shiny or novel things and may spend spontaneously when the opportunity arises. You may be more interested in learning the details and consider the full cost (over the long-term) for larger purchases, and your record-keeping may be quite creative.

Those who are less open to experience and more comfortable with the familiar may be less influenced by persuasive advertising and less likely to deviate from their weekly grocery list. The routine of buying an expensive morning coffee could be harder to break, and you prefer to take care of your highly organized record-keeping in private and on schedule.

How does your degree of openness to experience show up in your money behaviours? Record your thoughts.

## Self-Assessment Review

The more you know and understand about yourself, the better you are able to monitor and adapt your own behaviours. Also, the more you understand about personality traits in general, the better equipped you are to understand and consider the behaviour of others, in both your personal and professional settings.

The following questions will help you to consider how your personality influences your money behaviours.

* How congruent are your money behaviours with your primary, or dominant, general personality traits?

* Does your money style have a personality of its own?

* Are there any traits that seem to be more situational? If so, how does a situation influence those money behaviour/personality traits?

* How do your beliefs influence your money personality?

* How does self-control come into play in your general and your money personalities? Do you consider self-control more or less challenging for you than others?

* How do your money personality traits materialize in social situations?

* Does your money personality make you more susceptible to marketing influences?

There are many assessments available, but be cautioned that any personality assessment should only be interpreted with the assistance of a qualified and certified professional.

## Learn More about Your Unique Money Personality

Kathleen Gurney, PhD, specializes in financial psychology. Dr. Gurney suggests that "recognizing your own financial personality enables you to stop spinning your wheels of fortune and take charge of managing your money."[20] Dr. Gurney has been researching and studying the way Americans earn, spend, save, and invest their money for more than two decades and has developed a money personality profile assessment. Through her research, Dr. Gurney has identified how thirteen specific traits act as assets and some as liabilities to your personal financial style—knowledge that is key to understanding your unique money personality.

*Learn your own unique Financial Personality at a discount promotional price at BrokeFreeForever.com*

## ■ Appraising the Family Pedigree

You didn't grow up in a vacuum, oblivious to money or how your family handled it. You were influenced by the way your parents spent, the things they purchased, and the way they talked about money. If your parents didn't talk to you about money or spent recklessly, you may have grown up with little understanding of the true value of money. If times were tough when you were young, you may have matured into an adult who worries constantly about being without.

Here are some general questions to get you thinking about the money management environment you grew up in. Check the choice that most accurately represents your family.

— Money was handled wisely and discussed openly in my family.

— Money was handled wisely but never discussed in my family.

— Money was handled badly and openly discussed.

— Money was handled badly and never discussed.

*This doesn't give you an excuse to blame your mother or father!* Identifying the financial environment you grew up in may help you recognize some of your money behaviours, so you can take control and manage your own money wisely.

It might also be beneficial to think briefly about how your family's attitudes and behaviours were influenced by culture, nationality, religion, and even political affiliation. Take some time to consider how each of these influences might contribute to your own money behaviours.

**Show me your friends, and I'll show you your future.**

Teenagers aren't the only ones who go to great lengths to look and act like everyone else. Even adults are most comfortable as members of a like-minded group. This is due to an inherent human need to belong. While academic research is lacking on the subject, it is a widely held belief that the need to belong is hardwired through evolution into the survival of the human species. As cavemen and women, we hunted and cooked in groups. Being part of a group meant shared workloads and increased protection from outside threats. Because this inherent need to belong is strongly linked to personal survival, it stands to reason that social pressure, or peer pressure, can exert a strong influence on our choices and behaviours.

The relevant question then is: how do your friends and acquaintances influence your attitude towards money?

Considering the behaviours and attitudes of those people we spend time with, or who present themselves as role models, can serve to benchmark our own behaviours.

## ■ 'Cause I Said So!

Another external influence on money behaviour is marketing. In its simplest form, marketing is the activity of communicating to consumers; it is communication that is targeted to a specific market and intended to influence the consumer within that target market to make a buy purchase decision.

Marketing is designed to encourage us to purchase and spend. Pressure on consumer spending has never been greater. Marketing messages become more sophisticated, elaborate, and appealing as the range of advertising media increases. Huge amounts of money are spent to get your attention and your dollars while the shopping experience has become increasingly more convenient. The advent of online shopping, television shopping channels, social media, PayPal technology, and e-mail money orders, not to mention the availability of credit, has made spending more convenient and socially encouraged.

Marketers consider and design their communications based on a huge variety of factors, and a lot of consideration is given to brain functioning (neurology) and human behaviour (psychology). Communications include not only the words that we read or hear, but also what we see, feel, and experience, directly or indirectly. Here are some examples:

* Physical placement of items, such as a loaf of bread placed at eye level versus another brand placed on a lower shelf where you would have to bend over to look at it; competing coffee shops or gas stations kitty-corner across the street; brand-name props in a movie (the actors aren't drinking Coke or Pepsi by coincidence!)

* Timing of the day, week, or season or to align with local or national events, such as late-night shopping channel promotions or infomercials; advertising for humanitarian donations following an earthquake; or cheaper midweek airline tickets or hotel rooms versus weekend rates. Consider the flyers you receive at various times in the year. Marketers will remind you of their offerings right about the same time your mind is open to the concept of spending some money; this is all part of the increasingly fierce competition for consumer dollars. That is why you see jewellery and lingerie flyers in early February (Valentine's Day), office and school supplies and clothing for kids in August (back-to-school), costumes and candy in September (Halloween), and Santa Clauses and Christmas trees abound on store shelves and in the media before all the sticky remnants of the Halloween candy are washed away from tiny hands.

* Emotional experiences like wanting to protect or show how much we love our families, such as Hallmark card's tagline "when you want to send the very best" or protecting "what matters most" with the right insurance.

* Endorsements of real or perceived role models that a specific market might want to imitate, such as celebrities, sports personalities, and political figures, even personally influential figures or ideas (family, patriotism, the environment, etc.). Think Debbie Travis interiors or Elizabeth Taylor perfume.

Awareness of the powerful influence of marketing messages can be helpful when trying to regulate and control spending. "You can have it all!" many advertisers claim, and it's true. *But*, if you're like most people, you probably can't have it all *right now*. And those neighbours who do have it all, they just may be deep in debt.

# ■ Summary of Module 2

In this module, we considered our own personalities, as well as our friends and our family. Personality profilers help you identify, recognize, and celebrate your similarities and differences with your "peeps in your hood" in order to increase self-awareness and understanding. We also considered the market environment that we spend in.

## Money-Boosting Strategies from Module 2:

Strategy #4:  Be aware of your own unique complex personality and how it influences your decisions and behaviours.

Strategy #5:  Be aware of who has influence over your money behaviours.

## Access these Module 2 exercises and resources at BrokeFreeForever.com:

Personal Beliefs
Extreme Reality
Public Displays of Behaviour
Big Five Personality Traits
Financial Personality Profile Assessment
Reflection Questions

# Module 3:
## Onwards and Upwards!

***Go confidently in the direction of your dreams! Live the life you've imagined.***

—Henry David Thoreau

## ■ What Does Your Castle Look Like?

A man and his wife were vacationing in Rome. They came upon a huge work site where a number of bricklayers were working. They wondered aloud what they were building. The man approached one of the bricklayers and asked him, "What are you doing?"

The bricklayer replied, "I'm laying bricks!"

That didn't satisfy the couple's curiosity, so they went to the next bricklayer and asked him the same thing. The next bricklayer replied, "Ahhhh, you see, we're building a castle," as he gestured with his hands towards the massive site.

The difference between those two bricklayers was their vision. One was doing a job; the other was helping to build a castle—he held a bigger vision.

It is difficult to achieve something without having a clear idea of what it is. That is why I've devoted this module to creating a complete blueprint for your lifetime vision. Taking your vision from the abstract to the concrete requires step-by-step focused planning. This module is designed to help you turn your vision into logical, manageable goals and practical action plans.

Just like a contractor carefully surveys his site before building, it makes sense to survey your current financial situation before constructing your new plan.

## Snapshot of Your Financial Life

The following exercise is designed to help you determine your satisfaction level with your current status in a number of different areas.

Feel free to add any of your own line items in addition to those included. Rate each area on a scale of 1 to 5, where 1 indicates serious work required and a 5 indicates things couldn't be better.

— Income level—I am earning an adequate income for my lifestyle.

— Essential debt level (necessary items)—I know how long it will take me to pay off my debt. I have a plan.

— Nonessential debt (unnecessary items)—I know how long it will take me to pay off my debt. I have a plan.

— Debt expense—I know how much each of my debts costs me in fees, interest, and opportunity.

— Savings for expenses—I plan for and am not surprised by annual expenses.

— Savings for spending—I plan for and have funds to pay cash for vacations and holidays.

— Emergency fund—I have a contingency fund in case of emergency.

— Spending self-control—I stick to a plan/budget and do not impulsively blow my budget.

— Short-term goals—I have achieved and frequently achieve short-term financial goals.

— Long-term goals—I have achieved and frequently achieve long-term financial goals.

— Record-keeping—I can easily find receipts and transaction records.

— Monitoring—I keep track of my money coming in and going out.

— Credit rating—I have reviewed my credit rating within the past year and know where I stand.

Now that you have a better view of your point "A," let's start to consider the point "B" of your desired personal financial position.

## ■ Building Your Own 20/20 Vision

What do you want to achieve in your lifetime? What are your big-picture goals? Freedom? Security? Ownership? Peace of mind? A happy family life? Excitement? Developing hobbies and talents? A comfortable retirement? Travel? Education? Making the world a better place? There are so many things to aspire to.

As you prepare to develop a list of your own goals that build towards your lifetime vision, consider the following guidelines:

1.  A goal must be something you truly want or desire; otherwise, it's someone else's goal, not yours. While advice from others can be valuable, your goals should come from you, not your family, friends, peers, or societal pressure.

2.  A goal must be something you can realistically do, have, or be. Your lifetime vision represents an ideal, the best possible outcome for your life based on your resources and your reasonable expectations for increased income.

3.  A goal must be under your control. There is no sense in creating a goal that you have no control over. For example, redistributing the world population to better share resources is a great dream—but it isn't a goal. Rotating the moon so that we can better see what's on the other shady (dark) side would be cool—but it isn't a goal you can control.

4.  A lifetime goal may change. Goals are not written in stone. While they serve a purpose as a point of destination, goals are fluid. Consider the mountain theory of goals. As you set out on your journey to achieve a goal, just like climbing a mountain, your vision changes along the way. As your

vision changes, your knowledge increases and your perspective grows. You become aware of more options, and your choices may change the path you are on. Because of this, you may choose to change your goals. It is possible that the money you put aside for a summer on the nude beaches of Southern France ends up reallocated to your children's education fund or to the purchase price of a lakeside cottage.

5.  Values and circumstances change as we do, so it's possible that your ideas about who you are and what you want may undergo massive revision. And that's *okay*. In fact, it's great! The idea is to always have a vision in mind. Your vision…nobody else's!

So don't put too much pressure on yourself to come up with perfect goals—any goal that you set is right and good.

Take a few minutes to envision your most inspiring life. Use a blank sheet of paper to record words or phrases (or draw pictures!) that describe your *lifetime vision*.

## Prevention or Promotion—What's Your Focus?

When we focus on some goal that we want to achieve, we all have a natural lean towards one of two ways of thinking. Some people are *promotion-based*; that is, they describe their goals from the perspective of being advancing, achieving, or acquiring. Others are *prevention-based*; they describe their goals from the perspective of security, responsibility, and obligations. Neither of these is more important or "better" than the other, and just because you describe your objective in one way does not preclude that the other is also important to you.

Two professors have conducted research into how a prevention or promotion focus impacts our choices when we are making a purchase.[21] They used the example of two friends both in the market for a new car. One of them was single, lived in a warm climate, and had no children or dependents. She believed that life should be lived without regrets and planned to travel the open road in luxury and comfort. She had worked hard and now had the money for a new vehicle. When she visited friends and family, she wanted them to know she "had arrived." Her primary focus when choosing a car was on comfort and style; she wanted air-conditioning and GPS technology. On the other hand, her friend lived in a northern climate with her two children. She had also worked hard and now had the money for a new vehicle. She also wanted comfort and small luxuries like heated seats and GPS, but her primary focus was security and safety in case of an accident. She also wanted sidewall air bags and On-Star® communication technology. Who is promotion-focused, and who is prevention-focused?*

Consider this as you create your own goals, especially if you are developing mutual goals with a partner, spouse, family member, or friend. Though your initial goals might *appear* different, you might be working to the same end but stating the goal differently.

One partner may focus on saving for emergencies so an un-expected expense doesn't interrupt paying the mortgage (pre-vention-focused), while the other might focus on saving for an emergency so that the funds are available to take advantage of an opportunity (promotion-focused). Even if you seem to be on a different page for your goals, you could be in virtual agreement—agreeing on the same end goal, but getting there in a different manner, or for different reasons.

### Upping the Ante; Add Some Passion

To add some passion to your goals, describe *why* each goal is important to you. How will it change the way you feel or the way you experience life? Consider the impact your achieving this goal may have on others, and why that is important. Record whatever is relevant to you.

### Details, Details

The process of developing an action plan involves bringing your larger ideas into sharper focus by adding details. For example:

* ❁ "Travel" could be "Travel to the Cayman Islands for a month of Scuba Diving before I'm fifty."

---

* The first friend wanted people to know she "had arrived" and was successful. She chose her vehicle with a promotion-based focus. The second friend had a prevention-based focus of safety and security.

* "A happy family" could be written as "Buy a comfortable home with a yard in a neighbourhood close to a school by 2015."

* "Comfortable retirement" could be written as "having enough investments to provide a monthly annuity payment of $2,500 per month."

Write out your top three to five lifetime goals, with detail.

## Focusing Your Goals

A goal must be as specific as possible (write, revise, rewrite). No matter what your lifetime goals are, the sure way to achieve them is through a step-by-step change process.

Because you are the architect and the head contractor of your personal castle, it's your responsibility to develop a logical set of plans and a time line before you even start. This means breaking your lifetime goals into doable chunks. These chunks are the foundation of your lifetime goals; they are the incremental goals that lead up to the larger lifetime goals. We refer to these as *milestone goals*.

For each one of your lifetime goals, develop specific milestone goals and an action plan using the steps that follow.

**Note:** A widely practiced set of guidelines for goal setting is the SMART model. Consider this model as you develop your Milestone Goals.

**S**pecific—The more specific your description, the easier it is to develop your plan of action. Use specific numbers, names, dates, and any other effective descriptors wherever possible.

**M**easurable—Quantities, numbers, and values all make it possible to measure your progress.

**A**chievable—While we would like to believe that anything is possible, it may not be possible to triple your income this year, sell your home for double the market value, or convince your credit card provider to lower your interest rate to the Bank of Canada's base rate (kind of like a wholesale rate for interest).

**R**ealistic—You must be able to rely on reasonable expectations for current or future resources and be rational. Not everyone can sell their software company to Disney for hundreds of millions of dollars.

Time-sensitive—Time frames can vary from years to months to weeks to days—even hours! (Anyone who has quit smoking knows this!) A time frame adds perspective and positive pressure to your goals. Working backwards from your lifetime goals, pick milestone goals and dates that will help you organize your time line.

## Monitor and Reflect

Remember the mountain theory of goals? Because your action plan will reveal new information and lead you to new people and maybe even to new destinations, you may need to make adjustments. You will know this when you monitor and reflect on your progress.

Build a monitoring mechanism into your goals. This can be something as simple as a daily journal, checking items off a list, placing marbles in a jar or checking your monthly bank statements. As you monitor your progress, reflect on the original goals to ensure you are still moving towards that goal. Consider if you need to make adjustments to the next step or phase of your action plan or to the goal itself! Do you need to change directions? Solicit some professional advice? Track down a contact or resource? So long as you are doing something, you are probably heading in the right direction.

## And the award goes to...

A very important step in achieving your goals is to reward good behaviour and celebrate your successes. Of course, your rewards shouldn't counteract your goals. If one of your goals is to reduce spending, then buying the new socket wrench or hot knee-high boots may not be a good reward choice!

Symbolic rewards are rewards that affirm success but have little impact on budget. In a group setting, the symbolic reward could go to the member who reached or exceeded his or her monthly goal. Individually, a symbolic reward might be something that serves as a reminder of your progress towards a lifetime or milestone goal.

The feeling of success that accompanies updating a net worth chart to show the arrow on an upward (climbing) angle may be enough for some. For others, a reward could be splurging on an inexpensive purchase (if the budget allows!) or it could also be a certificate, a card, or something else that doesn't cost any money. The idea is to invest the reward with value by allowing the reward to represent long-term goals. It's kind of like playing a sport. Think about two hockey teams fighting over the puck. They will do anything to get that five-dollar piece of rubber because it represents something larger than itself. It has been vested with psychological (and in some cases monetary) value.

There are many ways to celebrate and reward your progress towards your goals. You can plan a special celebration, an event, a special treat (a Saturday morning latte when you have gone all week without), or give yourself a day off to watch movies in your pyjamas until noon. A day at the beach or in the backyard with a bottle of bubbles works too!

When you are creating your action plans, consider what milestones, dates, or progress proportions (such as a specific percent of a monetary goal achieved) might serve as appropriate reward/celebration milestones. You might even want to acknowledge an adjusted plan based on the new information resulting from good research!

The following examples are only that—examples. Depending on your own lifetime and milestone goals, your action plans may be much more, or less, detailed.

### Example Lifetime Goal #1:

Own my own home—mortgage free within thirty years. *Why Important:* To start building personal equity; to have my own personal yard and my own piece of the earth.

*Now break this lifetime goal into* **milestone goals** *and then each milestone goal into specific actionable steps required to achieve that goal.*

**Step 1—Milestone Goal #1**: Planning for a twenty-five-year mortgage, I will need to buy my own home within five years.

**Step 2—Action Steps to Achieve**: Within five years, have $10,000 saved to use for the down payment and purchase costs. To accomplish this, I need to:

* Save $147 per month at an estimated 5% annual interest rate.

* With a current budget of $30 per month going into savings, I need to find another $117 per month to contribute. I can:

- Increase my income by $117/month by:
  - Picking up two extra shifts
  - Taking on a paper route (and get my exercise too!)
  - Selling some of my hobby work at the farmer's market
- Decrease my expenses/spending by $117/month by:
  - Eliminating my credit card debt (current monthly payment is $150)
  - Eliminating my daily (workday) $6 morning coffee
  - Giving up one of my phone lines
  - Parking my car for the summer and taking the bus or bike

Action Steps This Week:

1. Call farmer's market to find out how to reserve a booth and the cost. *Note: make sure to deduct any added costs to earning this income in your overall calculation. You will need to earn enough to cover the costs and earn the extra income you need.*

2. Ask supervisor if I can pick up any extra shifts.

3. Make my own coffee at home. I will place my travel mug on the kitchen counter as a reminder.

4. Get bike from storage unit; check when car insurance expires.

5. Start a "Buy my own house" piggy bank / jar. Deposit all money saved/earned towards this goal into that bank at the end of each week (and then make a monthly deposit into the savings account!).

**Step 3—Monitor/Reflect/Adjust**: I will record my progress daily in my journal, calculating what I have saved by making my own coffee and approximate savings from riding my bike. At the end of this week, I will review this list and adjust the steps for next week as necessary.

### Example Lifetime Goal #2:

Enjoy a comfortable retirement by being financially independent. *Why Important:* I don't have any pensions or subsidies to rely on, other than Canada Pension Plan/Social Security old-age security benefits.

**Step 1—Milestone Goal #2 (A)**: Determine monthly savings requirement now based on reasonable and average rates of return and inflation values.

**Step 2—Action Steps to Achieve**: Enquire with financial planner to determine most appropriate retirement savings accounts, such as tax-free savings, registered retirement, or investment or other growth account.

Action Steps This Week:

1.  Call three financial planners and make appointments to meet them to determine which one I want to work with.

2.  Gather all documents necessary, including most recent pension plan statement, list of all liabilities, and income in preparation to meet with financial planner.

**Step 3—Monitor/Reflect/Adjust**: What have I learned from my financial planner that I need to do? What are my next steps?

*Sometimes, this step 3 is just taking a few minutes (or hours) to review where you are at and then making the next action plan steps for the following time period (week/month/quarter...).*

**Step 1—Milestone Goal #2 (B)**: Reduce my debt load, starting with most expensive debt first, and reallocate current monthly debt payments to retirement fund as available.

**Step 2—Action Steps to Achieve:** Calculate time to pay off all current debt based on existing annual interest rates and budgeted allocation of income towards debt repayment. Create a priority repayment plan based on current cost of debt.

Action Steps this week:

1.  Record all debts owing, including principal and interest rates and other pertinent information.

2.  Phone my friend Pamela and ask her if she will help me create a repayment plan (she has a financial calculator and knows how to use it). This plan will help me to set time

lines for repayment of my debt, giving priority to the most expensive debt first.

3. Create a new budget based on the debt repayment plan and reduce my spending by $200 to allocate towards debt repayment.

Possible spending reductions include:

❀ Reduce fuel spending—I will ride my bike to work three days per week to save approximately $70 per month.

❀ Reduce impulse spending—I will reduce my weekly cash-in-pocket spending amount from $60 to $40 per week, saving approximately $86 per month.

❀ Reduce utility spending—I will turn off lights, wash clothes in cold water, pay bills on time, clean my furnace filter, and keep my apartment two degrees cooler, in order to save $20 per month.

❀ Reduce my monthly grocery bill by the remaining $24/month goal. I will do this by buying more bulk foods, wasting less fresh produce, and doing comparison shopping. I will make a list for my weekly grocery trip to eliminate spontaneous spending.

**Step 3—Monitor/Reflect/Adjust**: I will record, on a daily basis, my spending and whether I used my car or my bike to get to work. I will estimate my savings on groceries by comparing with the average of my last three trips to determine how much I saved. I will write out my plan for next week, incorporating any adjustments that need to be made for further spending reduction.

### Example Lifetime Goal #3:

Increase my annual earnings by 30 percent. *Why Important:* My earnings don't provide an emergency fund or vacation spending. With the amount I'm making, I don't feel comfortable about the future. I can't afford holidays and worry about unexpected expenses. I never seem to have money to save.

**Step 1—Milestone Goal #2**: Determine options for retraining or career path opportunities by June.

## Step 2—Action Steps to Achieve:

1.  Attend introductory trade workshop at local college. Call to find out when next session is.

2.  Make appointment with free career path discovery centre through local government agency. Access their resources to determine strengths and define skills to assist in determining career options.

3.  Determine funding options through employment insurance, scholarship programs, and student loans. By the end of this week, make three phone calls to start enquiries and research.

**Step 3—Monitor/Reflect/Adjust**: By the end of this week, I will recap what I have learned from my research. Using this information, I will make an action plan for next week to identify three potential funding sources and acquire application forms or packages.

## Now It's Your Turn

For each lifetime goal, record the corresponding milestone goals and then outline the action steps you will need to take to achieve your first twelve-month goal. You might want to get a fresh piece of paper for each goal series and action plan.

## Why write goals?

Research has shown that the decisions you make on a daily basis are influenced by your long-term goals *when your attention is drawn to an anticipated emotion: pleasure or pain*.[22] Remember Sandy (payday pleasure)? When Sandy focused on her desired long-term goal, her urge to spend in the present was reduced significantly.

Short-term pleasures are necessary and deserved, but not at the sacrifice of long-term planning, as in the case of Janice. Janice's focus on immediate pleasure and her lack of understanding of its consequences exposed her to the possibility of long-term pain. Recognizing and embracing our desires for future pleasure can motivate us to take actions to avoid pain and experience pleasure. Writing out our goals, making them *visible*, is the first step toward seeing them as realities rather than daydreams. The more detailed our plans become, the more we enter into the new reality we are creating.

# ■ Summary of Module 3

Buying lottery tickets and befriending your aging aunts and uncles is one way to hedge your financial bets. But if you really want to take control of your financial future, *you need to control the management of your mind and your money, starting* now.

Module 3 focused on developing your personal vision for your future—your own castle. Translating your vision into milestone and actionable goals requires much planning. This module assists you to consider the important factors of setting achievable goals, using the SMART model mountain theory of goal setting. Additionally, this module focused on adding passion and details to your goals, monitoring and reflecting on your progress, and celebrating your achievements along the way.

## Money-Boosting Strategies from Module 3:

Strategy #6:    Have a lifetime vision.
Strategy #7:    Understand your prevention or promotion focus.
Strategy #8:    Write down your goals.
Strategy #9:    Create an action plan for every goal.
Strategy #10: Reward thyself!

## Access these Module 3 exercises and resources at BrokeFreeForever.com:

Financial Snapshot
Lifetime Goal Planning
Reflection Questions

# Module 4:
# Money 101—Back to Basics

*Teachers open the door, but you must enter by yourself.*

—Chinese Proverb

## ■ The Magic Formula

When it comes to having more money, there's no magic, but there is a simple formula: *always spend less than you receive and save or invest what is left over.* That's because incoming money *minus* outgoing money = seed money (a.k.a. live within your means).

Seed money is the money left over. Seed money represents possibility, because it can be divided between savings and investing—both of which are the seeds of growth.

Follow this formula, and you will live in a world of expanding possibilities. On the other hand, if you spend more than you receive, you'll be in a deficit situation, which forces you to beg, borrow, or steal to cover your debts. *(I'm joking about the stealing part!)* It's a simple logical concept that anyone can understand; yet, it is one that continues to baffle most of us.

## ■ A Closer Look at Incoming

Let's start with income; typically, that is money received or earned from any source. The key to creating a budget or plan that has the greatest probability of success is to work with the income you can plan for.

To break free from the payday-to-payday cycle, you need to construct a plan based on your regular sources of income (primary sources). Then, when you receive an irregular income amount (secondary source), you can allocate that money to debt reduction, savings, or investing, or whatever is at the top of your priority list.

Let's take a closer look at incoming:

## Primary

Primary income is the income that provides the most regular and predictable source of income. For most people, the most regular and predictable income comes from a salary or wages; others may receive a monthly pension amount, annuities from an investment, or even a regular payment from a court award or insurance payout.

## Secondary

Secondary income is other income you receive in addition to your primary income. This income may vary in amount, but it is predictable. Even if you hold a steady full-time job, some portions of your income may fluctuate based on certain travel or fieldwork allowances; a good month or a bad month for sales commissions, tips, and gratuities; or the payout of quarterly or annual bonuses.

The common denominator is that you **can predict** the receipt of secondary income (even if it is sporadic). As an example, sporadic secondary income could be generated by selling your belongings.

## Out-of-the-Blue Income

Out-of-the-blue income is unplanned and typically unexpected (although you are *hoping* for that lottery win!). The common denominator is that it is *not predictable*.

Frequency and duration of income will vary over the long term. Even if you hold a steady, full-time job, some portions of your income may fluctuate based on the time of season (i.e., a gig as Santa Claus at the mall or tips from guests at a tourist destination).

Of course, if you are self-employed, consistency of a steady income takes some thought.

## Self-Employment Income

Self-employment income merits some extra attention, because a little extra effort is required to plan for a regular and consistent stream of income—one of the keys to breaking free from the payday-to-payday cycle. If you are self-employed, you must pay yourself a regular income. Make your own wages a regular and ongoing expense and then budget your business income to pay that bill, just as you do with your other business expenses.

*Use the "Self-Employed Cash Flow" spreadsheet from BrokeFreeForever.com to plan your consistent income stream.*

If you are self-employed, how you pay yourself depends on whether you (and/or your partner(s)) operate your business as a sole proprietor or have an incorporated company.

As a sole-proprietor, you and your business are the same legal entity. All revenues earned less expenses may be considered as your income.

**In Canada,** as a sole-proprietor you still must pay Canada Pension Plan contributions on your income, as well as income tax. However; you are most likely not able to collect employment insurance (EI) and are therefore allowed to "opt out" of paying EI contribution payments. Legislation has changed recently so that some self-employed persons can contribute to and collect EI for certain situations. You may also need to pay the employer CPP and EI portions if you have employees. Be sure to check with a tax professional for current advice and rulings.

**In the United States**, as a sole-proprietor you must pay self-employment tax (SE tax), a Social Security and Medicare tax similar to that which is withheld at the source from employment wages. You may also need to pay excise tax or federal unemployment tax if you have employees. Be sure to check with a tax professional for current advice and rulings.

**If you are the shareholder of an incorporated company,** your company is considered a separate and legal entity, and the director/s (you or someone appointed by the shareholders) are the agent for its care. Any financial transactions between you and your company may have all kinds of tax implications, including income, federal and provincial or state taxes, and payroll deduction requirements.

**In the United States** if you are the sole member of your LLC earnings may be considered attributeable to you personally (as a Sole Proprietor) for income tax purposes. You should consult with a professional accountant and/or lawyer to ensure that your company is structured to accommodate your unique financial needs prior to incorporation.

Every province and state has its own corporate registry and legislation and regulations for conducting the affairs of the companies within that jurisdiction (or the federal registry for a federally incorporated company). Make sure you are familiar with your obligations and responsibilities as a director, as well as your rights as a shareholder.

Typically, you can receive money from the company in any number of ways, including as earnings (wages, salary or management fees), shareholder dividends, as shareholder loan (or other debt) repayments. Be sure to check with a tax professional for current advice and rulings, whether you are in Canada or the United States.

## Ways to Increase Income

### 1) Earn more money.

Every worker who trades his or her time for money is limited by the number of hours he or she is available to work and the amount he or she is paid per hour. In order to earn more, a worker must either *work more hours* or *earn more per hour*.

It's simple math that's anything but simple. Every hour you work is one less hour you have to spend with family and friends, so for many of us, working more hours is simply not an option. In that case, lobbying for a salary increase or applying for a higher paying job may be the only way to get ahead financially.

Consider other options as well, including retraining to gain more highly valued skills or moving to an area where the skills you have are more highly valued.

⌘ ⌘ ⌘

### True Story: Making the Change

Julie and her kids wanted to upgrade from their cramped two-bedroom apartment to a spacious three-bedroom but couldn't afford to. Julie was a careful budgeter who kept her expenses to a bare minimum, so she knew that reducing her expenses would not supply the extra income required to improve her family's situation.

Julie knew she could get a second job or work an extra shift, but her kids needed her at home. A pay raise was out of the question, so the only option was to find a job that paid more.

Julie spent a few gruelling months applying for new jobs and going to interviews on her lunch break. Eventually, she landed a job she'd never have tried for—if her discomfort hadn't forced her to push past her insecurities. Of course, the new job meant she had to move to a smaller community one hour north. But the increase in wages and the decrease in rent was worth it.

Today, she's enjoying her new apartment, loving her new job, and saving for the future.

⌘ ⌘ ⌘

## 2) Clear out the clutter.

One way to boost your income temporarily is to sell (a.k.a. unload) valuable items that someone else might enjoy. One person's trash is another person's treasure! The electric guitar you've never picked up, the fix-it-up antique that you haven't fixed up, or the jewellery that you never wear—de-cluttering is good for the spirit; there's nothing quite as cleansing as a good garage sale. *But beware!* There are *two limits* on income earned by selling stuff you own:

1. *Your inventory*—You probably bought most of your stuff because you needed it. Pawning your belongings is a very short-term source of income! And, if you need to replace those items later, you will probably be spending more

money on the replacements than you would get from the sale. Add the cost of advertising and possibly delivering your goods, and the idea seems even less appealing.

2. *The market value*—I'm sorry to have to break it to you, but the market value (what someone is willing to pay) for your secondhand couch or DVD player is probably nowhere close to what you paid for it! If you absolutely must raise some quick cash by selling something that you own: remember these two words: *supply* and *demand*.

The greater the supply (the more available) and/or the lower the demand (fewer people are interested), the lower the price you will get for your item. For example, consider the value of a used mattresses (low demand—ew!) or a used couch (high supply). These are definitely low-value items.

Generally, selling your used items is a short-term fix, unless you really are just trying to get rid of clutter!

### 3) Think like an entrepreneur.

Think back to when you were a kid and would do almost anything to earn a few bucks—from collecting bottles to selling lemonade. Now tap into that enthusiasm and brainstorm ways you can make extra money today.

One of the easiest ways to be involved in a sideline business is through a direct sales company. These entrepreneurial opportunities allow people a chance to get into business gradually, without overwhelming financial commitment, prohibitive advertising costs, or quitting their day jobs. Before getting involved with direct sales, make sure the company is reputable, that you can stand behind the product, and that the company's expectations are suitable to your temperament and availability.

Another source of entrepreneurial income is a hobby business. Could you turn your passion for making jewellery, toys, or perogies into a secondary income? Think about teaching your special skills to others as a way to enrich your community and your bank account. Be creative, and remember, there are no shortcuts to anything worth doing. Plan and take the time to do whatever you do well.

⌘ ⌘ ⌘

## ■ A Closer Look at Outgoing

Where does it all go? Most of us know how much we earn *(T4 slips and W-2s are good for something)* but have only a vague idea where our money really goes. This lack of awareness leaves us vulnerable to invisible overspending, which can drain money from our wallets like a slow leak. That four-dollar latte seems like a harmless indulgence, until you realize you're spending ninety dollars a month—that's more than $1,000 a year at the coffee shop!

And that's just coffee. When you review your spending over a six-month period, you'll probably be surprised to see how much of your hard-earned money goes to pay for things you could easily live without.

### Know Where Your Money Goes

It sounds simple, but the reality is that most of us couldn't account for where all of our money is going. We know we buy groceries, go out with our friends, and fuel our cars, but how much we actually spend on each category is largely a mystery—one we've been more than happy to leave unsolved.

*You can't change what you don't know…So it's time to pull your head out of the sand and figure out just how much life is costing you.*

Start out each day with a set amount of pocket money. Knowing how much you started with (each day) will make it easier to remember where you spent that money.

At the end of each day, calculate how much money you have spent and take some time to remember what exactly you spent the money on. Write it down. It is very important to take those couple of minutes at the end of each day to record your daily spending since much of our spending can happen so effortlessly.

If you find it very difficult to remember, then you may need to take this task one step further. Use a worksheet to record *every penny* that you spend *every day* for the next four weeks. Record every cash, credit, or debit transaction no matter how small. Here are some ideas to help you remember:

* Get a receipt for *everything!* It is really easy to forget about the $2 muffin or the $1 newspaper purchase.

* Use a small notebook to keep a running tally of every penny (nickel and dime) you spend as you spend it.

At the end of each day, transfer the information from your receipts and/or notebook to a worksheet.

*Download a "Spending Tracker" worksheet from BrokeFreeForever.com.*

*Note:* It is very important when tracking your spending to take those couple of minutes at the end of each day to record the daily spending. This is much easier—and takes way less effort—than saving up your receipts to record at the end of a longer period. Just imagine a large shoe-box full of receipts at the end of the month; now that's ugly and no one wants to muddle through those! Chances are, you just won't do it. A couple of minutes a day is key!

## Example Tracking Headings

Mortgage
Rent
Natural Gas or Oil
Power/Electricity
Water
Cable or satellite service
Internet service
Land / Cell phone(s)
Strata or Condo fees
Other utilities / services
Personal loan(s)
Student Loan(s)
Automobile loan
Credit Card(s) balance
Private loan(s) owing
Automobile insurance
Banking fees
Bus / Taxi
Automobile Gas
Parking fees
Automobile maintenance (oil
changes, tires, annual service, etc.)
Life / Disability insurance
Health insurance
(basic and/or extended)
Alternative health care (massage,
chiropractor, physiotherapist, dentist)
Daycare / Babysitting
Clothing
(includes outerwear and underwear)
Dental and Eye care
Extra-curricular lessons & sports fees
Groceries – pantry staples
Groceries – household staples
Groceries – fresh produce
Groceries – freezer and fridge
consumables
Hobbies
Foot ware

Prescriptions
Hair cuts
Personal grooming
Lunches out
Coffee shops / snacks
Dinners out
Movies
Gambling
(including pull tabs)
Pubs / night clubs
Concerts
Sports activities – summer
Sports activities – winter
Holiday activities
Other entertainment
(include entertaining IN)
Travel & Holidays
Other recreation
Birthday gifts
Holiday gifts
Holiday decorating
Magazines & Newspapers
Alcohol
Maintenance
School fees
Tuition
Text books
Other Reading
CD's and DVD's
(purchase or rental)
Computer supplies & maintenance
(paper, ink)
Computers & Electronics (software &
games)
Dry cleaning and Tailoring
Lawn care and/or housekeeping
services (contractor)
Charity and Donations (such as
religious tithings)

Once you have a comprehensive list of where your money is going, consider which category each item falls into: essential expenses, nonessential expenses, debt repayment or spending for play and fun.

## Essential Expenses

These are must-haves – the basics to live by. This will include shelter, food, utilities, health care, some savings, etc. What is considered *essential* may vary from one person to another at different points in your life. But be reasonable. Ask yourself: "Do I *need* this or *want* this?"

## Nonessential Expenses

This includes all *voluntary* spending for things not included in the essentials category. Examples might include: designer clothing, cable television, Internet, a second phone service (or even the first!), club memberships, extracurricular lesson fees, and charitable donations.

## Debt Repayment.

Kind of self-explanatory, eh? Subcategorize your debt into essential and nonessential.

## Spending for Play and Fun

This spending is for things like entertainment, dining out, pocket money, gifts, and subscriptions, etc. There may be a fine line between this category and some nonessential expenses. Use your best judgement to categorize your spending in the way that makes sense for you.

### Variable Versus Fixed Expenses

Variable and Fixed expenses are common business terms used to categorize expenses as to whether those expenses are directly associated with earning sales revenues or occur with or without revenues. For example, the price a business owner pays for an inventory item or the commissions they pay to a salesperson are *variable* expenses; they are a direct cost of making that sale. A fixed expense is something you pay whether you make any sales or not, such as rent, insurance, salaries, and utilities. If you are comfortable with the idea of fixed and variable expenses, you can use these in your own personal budgeting plans. I don't use them in this book because I consider *all* personal expenses to be fixed in the short term and variable in the long term. We all have the control to change any personal expenses (including mortgage, rent, debt, or utilities) by making choices and changes. Sure, some things may take longer to change, but if you have to cut expenses, then you can choose to buy a cheaper car or move to a cheaper neighbourhood.

## Ways to Reduce Expenses

Most people do not want to cut back on the things they enjoy most. If you are an avid socialiser, a fashionista, a foodie, a techie, or a committed movie buff, the idea of cutting back spending on your special passion might strike you as about as much fun as cutting off one of your legs. So let's start the easy way and cut back on the things that have the least impact on your lifestyle.

## 1) Utilities

You can save over a hundred dollars a year by reducing utility expenses. Reduce your utility bills by $10 a month, and you will save $120 a year! Here are some ideas for reducing your utility consumption:

* Turn off lights when you leave the room—and even in the room you are in!
* Use energy-efficient lightbulbs.
* Wash laundry in cold water.
* Turn down the furnace. (Put on a sweater instead of cranking up the heat!)
* Clean or replace filters on your furnace, fans, and vacuum cleaners.
* Don't let the water run while washing the dishes or brushing your teeth.

Talk to your utility supplier about setting up equal monthly payments to keep your payments from fluctuating with the variation in how much you use. Many companies offer this option once you have been a customer for at least one year. Having regular monthly payments makes budgeting easier.

If you had to pay a deposit when you first opened your utility account, find out if you can have that money returned. Some utility companies keep the deposit until you close your account, but some only require a deposit for the first year. Check to see if and when you can have your deposit returned.

## 2) Pay on time.

Avoid paying unnecessary fees and penalties by paying your bills on time! Every time you pay a bill late, you not only might be hurting your credit rating, you are giving away your hard-earned money needlessly by having to pay late fees or interest on over-due amounts. (If you *really* don't care about your money, send it to me! I'd be happy to have it!)

As a general rule, pay all of your bills *at least three days before they are due*. Why three days? Because if you pay your bills elec-tronically (online or via telephone banking), it could take three business days for the transaction to be recorded. Just being one day late could add interest or penalty fees to your bill. A 10 per-cent penalty adds up quickly—as do interest charges!

To avoid the end-of-the-month crunch, consider any bills or expenses due in the first two weeks of any month as being due at the end of the previous month. When you are using the My PayDay Budget system (Module 8), your bills/expenses should automatically come out of your bank account when due so that you will never pay late fees or interest penalties. Keep your money; don't give it away!

## 3) Pay cash.

Many of us grew up expecting and receiving instant gratifica-tion. If we wanted new shoes, someone bought them. If we needed a holiday, we just went with little thought as to how or when we'd pay for the trip. If as children we begged for something in the mall, chances are we went home with it. Easy access to credit has made it too easy for us to walk into a store and walk out with a couch, television, or computer that we don't need and can't afford.

How can you remedy this? *Use cash.* By using your own money to purchase items you want or need, you avoid paying the as-sociated costs that come with borrowing money (see the "Psssst! Wanna Buy a Loan?" module).

Also, when you pay with cash, you might even get a better dis-count! Just because the price is printed on a sticker doesn't mean that's the price you have to pay. On a big-ticket item, always make an offer—even in a department store. Ask for the manager or supervisor. You have worked hard for your money, so don't give it away too freely. Businesses have to pay a percentage of the item's value of every credit card transaction they process (and they pay a fee for debit card transactions too). These are fees paid to their merchant services provider: the company that processes the credit and debit card transactions. These percentages can range from 1.5 to 3.5 percent or more! So, if you can pay for your purchase in cash, negotiate for a 2 to 3 percent discount on the total price. After all, you will be saving the business from paying that same expense—better in your pocket than theirs!

**Consider this**: If you want to pay for a $1,700 purchase on credit, at 2.9 percent, that store will pay their merchant services provider $49.30. If you pay cash, haggle for the equivalent discount and you also save the associated tax. At a 5 percent tax rate you are now saving $51.77. That could go towards your groceries, a credit card statement, or even pay for a night out at the movies! Go ahead; you deserve it for being money-wise!

## 4) Reduce impulsive spending.

Grocery shopping can be expensive when you don't plan ahead; making extra (midweek) trips to the store will frequently result in buying unplanned (and unnecessary) items. It is not unusual to pay more at the convenience store close to home than at a larger discount store. While it is great to support local small business, when you are trying to reduce expenses, shopping at a discount store may make more sense, as long as it's not too far away. Here are some more grocery-shopping money-saving tips:

* Don't shop for groceries when you're hungry!
* Buy in bulk when nonperishable items are on sale—Look for case lot sales. You can always find a friend who might be willing to split the case and share the savings.
* Use coupons whenever possible. Just be careful, sometimes the price of a name-brand item (even with the coupon) is still greater than a store-brand or no-name-brand item.

## 5) Remove (or at least watch out for!) bundled services.

Cable and cell phone companies are perfect examples. Do you *really* need to spend the extra $5 per month or $15 per month for bundled services? Even though you will be saving $4 per month by bundling the call-waiting, voice-mail, and call-forwarding features instead of paying separately for them, consider whether you really need them. Instead of saving $4 per month by bundling all three services (and then only paying $10 per month for all three), try skipping them altogether! You will then save yourself $10 per month—or $120 per year (plus the associated taxes).

If you are one of those people who has all the bells and whistles on your cell phone, keep track of how much you actually use them. Are you paying for bundled data usage to access the Internet from your cell and then only using it once or twice a month? By changing how you communicate (checking your e-mails once/twice a day instead of as they come in), you can cancel your cell-phone data service and save yourself a lot of money.

How much are you paying for your television service? Do you really need all of those channels? What would happen if you disconnected your cable for a year and only rented movies (or watched online)? Do the math—and then prioritize. What do you need more, the extra $35 per month (that's $420 per year you can put towards your debt, investments, or vacation) or the security of knowing that you can watch a repeat of *Top Gun* for the seventh time? Just for fun, try this "Television Cost Cruncher" exercise.

Track the time you spend watching television (in half-hour increments) for the next week:

Sunday _____ Monday _____

Tuesday _____ Wednesday _____    Multiply the Total Week by 52 for an annual Total:

Thursday _____ Friday _____

Saturday _____ **Total Week:** _____    _____ (a)

How much do you pay for your television (cable or satellite) service per month?    _____ (b)

Multiply (b) by 12 to determine the annual cost    _____ (c)

Divide the annual cost (c) by the total hours of viewing time above (a). **This is how much your television viewing time costs per hour.**    _____

How does that compare with how much you earn per hour?

## ■ Frugal—The *Good* F-word

Frugal is the new rich! Studies show the majority of millionaires got that way by living below—rather than at or beyond—their means. Being frugal is how their means increased!

While living within your means (not spending more than you have coming in) may be challenging now, as your wealth increases as a result of your "frugal" attitude, your lifestyle possibilities expand accordingly.

*Frugal* **is not a bad word!** Being frugal is not an indicator of being cheap or greedy. In fact, research shows that it's it the most reliable method of wealth creation. It's about making short-term sacrifices to achieve long-term goals.[23] A number of recurring themes among self-professed frugal consumers ("Frugalites") have been identified.

They practice restraint and discipline when purchasing and are resourceful in the use of their belongings (again, remember the marshmallow experiments?). Frugalites see themselves as:

* disciplined in spending

* generally less impulsive

* placing more emphasis on long-term gratification

* resourceful in using and reusing possessions (they acquire and pay for fewer possessions)

* more independent than the average person

* less susceptible to interpersonal influence

Frugalites tend to be motivated by long-term outcomes; they are future-oriented. They typically avoid impulse purchases or spending to satisfy immediate (or short-term) desires. Where do you think you fit in on the money-spending spectrum? Are you more likely to be disciplined and plan your spending or are you impulsive and spend your money easily?

### Seven Ways to Increase Your Frugalite Factor.

1. **Buy smarter.** When you take the time to research your purchase options (where to buy, when to buy), you increase

the likelihood of getting the best price. Many times, a little bit of research can save you money and future frustration. Here are two ways to conduct your research:

a. The "Decision Matrix Tool" (available for download at BrokeFreeForever.com) will assist you in making quality purchasing decisions for high-cost or specialty items. The Decision Matrix will help you to define the important features or specifications for the item you desire and then help you to rate your purchase options based on a rating scale. You can use the tool to compare the importance of any specific feature, including specifications, color, cost, warranty, or whatever might hold any degree of importance to you.

b. Shop around! Compare prices. Many stores now promise a "lowest-price" guarantee. The catch is that the item must be the exact make and model. So, after using the Decision Matrix to determine the make and model of the item you want, shop online, compare flyers, and even phone different stores to compare the prices for the item.

2. **Do the math.** Always take the time to consider how much a decision will cost you—in interest, lost opportunity, or convenience. If you need to borrow money to make a purchase, consider the cost of that money. A poor decision can cost you not only cash but also opportunity (see the "Psssst! Wanna Buy a Loan?" module).

3. **Dream. Delay. Design—Use a needs and wants list.** When you really want that item that you saw advertised, put it on your *dream* list. Then, *delay* the purchase for at least a week. During that time, you can consider whether you truly need or want the item, how you will pay for it, and if necessary, what you are willing to give up. If you are to proceed with buying the item, *design* a payment plan that fits your budget; for example, source funds you have allocated in the *Savings for Spending Account* in the My PayDay Budget ("Your Personal PayDay Plan" module). The idea is to avoid impulse buying or shopping out of boredom. By delaying your purchase, you will have an opportunity to shop around

(see #1). You may find a better deal at another store, or you may even find that the desire has passed, that you really didn't need or want the item.

4. **Buy used.** If you need something that you can buy second-hand, do so! If you need an appliance or a piece of furniture, start researching while you save for it. It is not uncommon to find great bargains if you take the time to look, especially for costly items, such as sporting equipment and furniture. Check out secondhand stores, consignment stores, and merchandise discounters. Go online! Many communities have online classified ads for items available at low cost, for barter/trade, and even for free!

5. **Cook your own meals.** By spending twenty to sixty minutes in the kitchen, you can create a healthy meal that costs (on average) anywhere from $2.00 to $6.00 per serving. The restaurant equivalent will cost you upwards of $14.00 for the same meal, and don't forget to add in the cost for coffee, taxes, and a 15 percent tip!

Most people reach for convenient prepared foods because of busy schedules and lack of time. There are gads of easy recipes that take less than thirty minutes to prepare and are healthier choices for both your physical being and your pocketbook! If you always make more than you need, you will have enough left over for lunch the next day and maybe even to put in the freezer for a quick dinner the next time you are running short of time. Make creating leftovers a new habit!

Cooking can also be fun and very creative. Share the chore with your family members, friends, and/or room-mates. Have progressive dinner parties on the weekends; make enough for two or three meals and freeze the left-overs.

Invest in a couple of practical cookbooks to expand your collection of meal ideas. There are many that offer quick and easy meal solutions using basic pantry ingredients. Some of my own personal favourites are published by *Company's Coming* and *Canadian Living*.

6. **Don't be wasteful.** Squeeze out the last drop! Many lotions and shampoos come in bottles with pump dispensers. When a dispenser seems empty, most people throw it out and buy a replacement. Instead, remove the dispenser and place the container upside down over a cup or another container to capture the remaining contents. With toothpaste, cut off the wide end and squeeze it out into a cup. You may be surprised how much is left over!

   The same goes for food. Start paying attention to how much is left at the bottom of the box, jar, container, bag when you throw it out or replace it because it's almost empty. All those last little bits really add up over time, resulting in money thrown away.

7. **Stop paying for things you don't need to.** Consider those things you are spending money on now that, with better time management or increased skills, you could do yourself!

   Housecleaning—Spend the extra ten to twenty minutes a day to clean as you go and the two to four hours every week for the bigger jobs, rather than pay an hourly wage to your housekeeper.

   Learn to sew—It only takes minutes to repair a lost button, repair a torn sleeve, or fix a dropped hem. Fixing often makes more sense than throwing away and/or replacing.

   Repairs— Learn to make minor furniture repairs with proper glues or nails and a hammer. Fixing the broken stool, chair, or table may be much cheaper than replacing it.

## ■ Summary of Module 4

In this module, we reviewed the basic math equation: incoming less outgoing = seeds of possibility. By building our personal plan on what we know to be regular and consistent (primary) income, we can focus on decreasing expenses and increasing our seeds of financial possibility.

### Money-Boosting Strategies from Module 4:

Strategy #11:  Do the math. Incoming less outgoing = possibility.

Strategy #12:  Identify your current and future income potential.

Strategy #13:  Know where your money goes, and what expenses you are tolerating.

Strategy #14:  Frugal is the new rich! Increase your Frugalite factor.

### Access these Module 4 exercises and resources at BrokeFreeForever.com:

Dream | Delay | Design

Self-Employment Cash Flow spreadsheet

Spending Tracking Weekly/Daily spreadsheet

Spending Tracking spreadsheet

Personal Monthly Spending Tracker spreadsheet

Decision Matrix

Reflection Questions

# Module 5:
# Pssssh! Wanna Buy a Loan?

*No debt ever comes due at a good time.*
*Borrowing is the only thing that seems handy all the time.*

—Will Rogers

## ■ The Good, the Bad, and the Ugly

*The best things in life are free*
*But you can keep 'em for the birds and bees*
*Now give me money, (that's what I want) that's what I want.*

Those lyrics have been sung by many artists since Barrett Strong first sang the tune in 1959.[24]

While money has not been around forever, the need to be able to track an exchange of value has been. Before coins were put into use, different commodities were used to keep track of economic exchange between people, including livestock, precious metals, gemstones, cubes of tea, shells, beads, feathers, slabs of salt, and even IOUs. Even during those pre-coin years, it was possible to owe more than you owned. Those people too had debt. So debt, in fact, has been around longer than money!

But despite the older-than-dirt history of debt, a *Harvard Business Review* article reports the results of a national research poll of one thousand U.S. consumers found that the majority of adults were not very debt literate.[25] That same article reports that U.S.

households have more than doubled their debt loads from the previous generation, and almost half of Americans responded that they "probably couldn't come up with $2,000 in thirty days" to meet an unexpected financial need.

Similarly, a consumer survey conducted by the Certified General Accountants Association of Canada reported that if the total 2009 household debt were evenly spread across all Canadians, the individual debt loads would be 2.5 times greater than in 1989 and that one-quarter of Canadians would not be able to handle an unforeseen expenditure of $5,000.[26]

So, this module is dedicated to everyone as a timely primer, or review, on the components of debt.

## Not all debt is created equal.

You may already be familiar with the concept of good debt and bad debt. I propose a third category: ugly debt. Ugly debt can put you into a deep, deep hole. This hole can quickly become a trap that is very difficult—and very expensive—to escape from.

### Good Debt

Good debt is that which helps you achieve a positive goal and in the long term increases your net value. It is *productive debt*; that is, you end up with more value even after the total cost of the debt has been factored in. For example: using debt to buy an investment that is expected to increase in value. That could include a house, vehicle, stock or fund investments, artwork, jewellery, and even precious metals or commodities.

Good debt can be used as *leverage*, that is, to provide the means to increase value elsewhere. This could be the purchase of equipment needed to operate a business (generate profits and earn income), or for investment in stocks or funds (with the idea of receiving future annuities or dividends). Sometimes you are entitled to use the interest you must pay on a debt as a tax or expense deduction. Check in with a trusted financial advisor to obtain advice specific to your personal situation.

Good debt could be used to purchase something that costs more than you can realistically save enough cash for, such as big-ticket furniture, appliances, or a vehicle. Of course, real-estate purchases typically fall into the good debt category.

The key to good debt is manageability. The total value of the money you borrow plus the cost of that debt should stay within a set maximum percentage of your total income and fit within your allotted budget.

A common measurement used in the financial industry to determine the weight of the debt load you are carrying is called the debt service ratio (DSR). This ratio is referred to as the handcuff margin in the "Personal Financial Performance Ratios" in the "Taking Stock" module.

### Bad Debt

Bad debt is typically any debt that grows in value (cost) while the value of what it was used for stays the same or decreases. In this case, you end up paying more than the value received. This typically includes consumables that are long gone before the debt is paid off (such as restaurant meals, alcohol, cigarettes, entertainment, and even vacations), or purchases that lose financial value faster than the debt is paid off, such as a new vehicle, a computer, or the latest electronic toy.

Debt is bad when you will end up paying more than the value you receive for it; you are *throwing your money away* by handing it over to someone else (the lender) without realizing any real value. Bad debt is *unproductive*. It is not working for you; it is working against you. Think of it like empty calories (calories you consume that don't give you any nutritional value!). The money you pay in fees and interest is the cost of the bad debt—and you aren't getting any value in return for it!

If you aren't living payday to payday, maybe you can afford to give your money away without realizing any value in exchange. If you are, then you might consider giving that excess money you have to a worthy charity or send it to me! As previously noted, I'd be happy to receive it! (I'm just saying…!)

You want to pay off and eliminate bad (empty) debt as quickly as possible, because then, you can refocus those funds towards repaying good debt or growing your savings and investments to grow your net worth.

## Ugly Debt

Ugly debt is like a vacuum. If you have debt that is costing you so much in fees and interest that you cannot afford to reasonably pay down the original amount borrowed (principal), you have ugly debt. This debt is ugly because the cost of a loan is calculated on the principal amount owing, if you cannot reasonably pay down that principal amount, you are in a cycle of giving your money away without having any positive effect for yourself—and not only are you not realizing any value, the total cost keeps growing!

⌘ ⌘ ⌘

### True Story: On Top of the World

John had held a steady job for the past three years. He was working in the gas industry and was making pretty good wages. Young and single, John liked to buy nice things and had lots of toys. He also ate out frequently at restaurants and had a few expensive habits. John loved to deck out his computer and his car and frequently used his credit card to buy things online. Before he knew it, John had maxed out several credit cards to the tune of $10,642.07.

With every paycheque, John was feeling the pressure. After meeting his other obligations (rent, utilities, car payment, and insurance), he wasn't making much more than the minimum payment and felt like he wasn't making any headway in paying off the credit cards. John felt it would be easier to manage this debt—and take the pressure off—if he consolidated all of his debt obligations into one loan.

A local financial company agreed to lend him the money and would even sell him some insurance coverage in case he lost his job and couldn't pay his loan payment. John accepted the loan terms, signed the loan agreement, and received his cheque. He felt ggrrreat! He now only had one loan payment to worry about in addition to his car payment and other living expenses. He was so proud that he called his mom to tell her how he had paid off his credit card debt.

When John showed his mom the loan agreement, she helped him to calculate what the total cost of this loan would be. The cost of the insurance ($2,650.62) was added to the $10,642.07 that he borrowed, for a total principal loan amount of $13,202.60.

John was shocked (and extremely freaked out!) when he went through the calculations with his mom and learned that he had agreed to pay back a total of $25,374.45 to pay off his original debt of $10,642.07.

With the 29.9 percent interest rate over four years, John had agreed to pay the finance company $12,171.85 in addition to the original borrowed amount of $10,642.07. Put another way, just the cost (fees and interest) of this loan was equal to two years of monthly payments of $475.25 per month. Now that's one ugly debt!

Here is how the amounts break down:

| | |
|---|---|
| Original debt | $10,642.07 |
| Additional fees | $2,560.52 |
| Interest (over term of loan) | $12,171.85 |
| Total paid | $25,374.45 |

How it turned out: John was very fortunate; his mom offered to provide the loan. John signed an agreement with his mom to pay off the loan at her line-of-credit interest rate of 5 percent. John and his mom visited the loan salesman and paid off the loan two days after John signed the original agreement. It cost John almost $100 in fees and interest to pay out the loan in full. Making the same monthly payment of $475.29, John paid off the loan from his mom in twenty-two months (just under two years instead of four). John cut up all but one of his credit cards—for good. (Thanks, Mom!)

⌘ ⌘ ⌘

While that example may seem to be a bit extreme, it's very real (and a true story!) and happens every day to unsuspecting debtors just trying to get ahead.

## A Closer Look at Consolidation Loans

To consolidate means to combine into a whole. When someone buys a consolidation loan, he or she borrows money from a lender to pay off a number of other creditors, in effect, turning all of those separate loans into one big one. This can be an effective option to get your financial house in order and provide some short-term relief, but if this method is not used wisely, it can set you back. A consolidation loan has the *potential* to fall into the ugly loan category. This practice can get you into hot water if you use the opportunity to increase your debt load by rounding up the amount you borrow (above and beyond the sum of the individual loans you are including) to pay for a new purchase, a vacation, or whatever. John (real life ugly debt story) found that out the hard way when additional fees were added to an extremely high interest rate (29.9 percent).

The trouble with consolidation loans is that the people who need them the most are typically people with a poor credit rating, large amounts of debt, and limited to zero assets. They are considered high-risk borrowers and typically have a very difficult time securing a low-interest loan from a traditional lender (bank). They often find themselves hit with high-interest rates and fees that land them back where they started—in debt over their heads.

Traditional lending institutions (with average interest rates) are more interested in lending money to people who are low risk and therefore less likely to forfeit on the debt. High-risk borrowers (those whose ratio of debt to income is high) are left to haggle with more predatory lenders.

It's a vicious cycle that sees people lured by a quick fix and then landing back where they started in as little as two years: in debt over their heads.

If you are seriously considering a consolidation loan, shop around to get the best interest rate and be sure to calculate the monthly payment over the term of the loan to consider how much you are really going to be paying. If you can afford to be patient, build up your credit worthiness (see the "Flirting with Your Banker" module) and seek out any other options you can find as an alternative to high-interest lenders.

If you are really deep in debt, be sure to read the "Help I'm Drowning in Debt!" section of this module.

## A Closer Look at Payday Loans

Payday loans offer easy access to quick money; payday lenders provide a service that is used by many individuals. Here's how they work. A nontraditional lender provides a short-term loan (typically ten days) to a person who needs money between paydays.

The borrower writes a post-dated cheque to cover the original loan amount, plus fees and interest. The payday lender then cashes the cheque at the end of the loan period. A 2007 government review reports payday loans are typically for less than $1,000 and the average loan value is about $280.[27]

A recent study considered the impact of payday loans on consumer insolvency: the situation where consumers who have much more debt than they can pay off go bankrupt. Researchers found that in 2006, 29.5 percent of bankrupt consumers owed more than 25 percent of their total household income to payday lenders.[28]

They also reported that while many consumers use these alternative lenders to help make ends meet between paydays, the danger exists when these loans are rolled over (refinanced) to the next payday, resulting in additional fees being levied and making these loans the "*most expensive source of consumer credit available*."

Here is an example of how that works. The following table shows details from an actual 2004 transaction included in the Berry and Duncan report:

| | |
|---|---|
| Value of the payday loan advanced on 09-27 2004 | $400.00 |
| Amount paid by the borrower on 10-14 2004 | $451.28 |
| Term of the loan | 17 days |
| Breakdown of amount paid by borrower: | |
| Principal | $400.00 |
| Interest | $8.64 |
| Per item fee | $9.99 |
| Cheque-cashing fees (7.99% of principal and interest) | $32.65 |
| Effective annual rate of interest | **1,242%** |

Payday loan interest rates and laws vary throughout Canada and the United States. In British Columbia, payday lenders must be licensed and cannot charge more than 23 percent interest on short-term loans. In Nova Scotia, lenders are able to charge as much as 31 percent while Manitoba caps the interest rate at 17 percent for loans of up to $500.[29]

The Consumer Federation of America (CFA) indicates payday loans are prohibited in sixteen states and the District of Columbia, because small-loan and interest-rate laws have been deregulated or exempted. Caps on interest rates reportedly vary up to 25 percent to 30 percent. Thirty-five states have maximum fee and interest caps that can reach as high as the equivalent of 572 percent annual percentage rate.[30]

The Canadian Payday Loan Association (CPLA) Web site sets out a code of conduct that its members must abide by. This code of conduct outlines that payday loans must not be rolled over and presents caps on overdue interest that can be charged and sets out that a lender may *not* "take an assignment of wages" or "threaten criminal action or use other forms of intimidation or harassment to collect outstanding amounts."[31] Visit the CPLA Web site (a link is included in the "Resources" section) for a list of CPLA registered members and other payday-loan industry information.

If you would like to find out the equivalent interest rate for payday loan fees, go to the simple online payday loan calculator listed in the resources section. Input the amount borrowed and the fee per $100, and the tool will calculate the equivalent interest rate. You might be amazed!

## A Closer Look at Buy Now / Pay Later

We've all seen them, those tempting glossy flyers that come in the mail with headlines screaming: "Pay Nothing for 18 months!" A "buy now, pay later" proposal is common for furniture and appliance dealers. And, just to make the pot a little sweeter, sometimes, they'll even throw in a "free 47-inch super-duper amazing flat-screen television" if you buy *now* (or this weekend).

The good news is, this can be a *great* option if you were planning to buy furniture or appliances anyway. It is a good debt opportunity because there is no interest!

A word of caution: this is *only* good debt if you pay off the total amount of your purchase *during the no-interest period*. Yes, that means you actually make payments during the no-payment period. If you don't, this good debt can quickly turn to bad debt or even ugly debt if you aren't careful. And don't forget to look for added fees; read the contract closely.

**Here's how it works.** When you purchase using this option, the documents you sign will indicate loan terms. You are actually agreeing to a loan. This may be disguised within the agreement as a third-party lender granting the loan as of the date the purchase amount becomes due.

The terms of the loan agreement *do* include interest, and maybe even fees. The catch is that you do not pay any interest if you pay off the total loan amount *on or before a certain date*. If you do not pay the amount off in full, interest begins accruing as of that date, and sometimes retroactively.

Depending on the lending institution (usually an alternative lender, otherwise known as a high-interest lender), interest could be any amount allowable by law—and usually is somewhere around 20 to 25 percent. I have seen agreements with interest terms as high as 29% (or more!). What's more, the interest is typically *retroactive*; that is, it is calculated beginning *from the date you purchased!* Suddenly, that free money is looking awfully expensive, and we haven't even considered the added fees yet.

Then, when your purchase is a year old (and maybe even worn out or broken), you could suddenly find yourself owing the original purchase price, *plus* a full year's worth of interest, *plus* administrative or other fees. This is beginning to look like ugly debt.

But don't throw away that glossy flyer yet! Buy now, pay later financing works when:

* You pay monthly instalments against the debt during the no-interest period; or

* You put the monthly payments into a savings account (hey, you may as well earn the interest!) and then pay the full amount owing a few days before it is due. Use caution here; having the money sitting available in a savings account could be pretty tempting!

The key is that you must pay off the amount before the due date so you do not incur interest and other fees. Tip: pay off the debt a few days or a week or so early; sometimes if the due date lands on a nonbusiness day, it could be calculated a day or two earlier. It is much easier to pay the amount due a few days earlier than try to have the interest and fee calculations reversed.

⌘ ⌘ ⌘

### True Story: What a Deal (Not!)

Gail walked into the local electronics store with $600 cash she'd saved to buy a laptop. She was heading towards models in her price range when she spotted the computer package of her dreams—and an offer she couldn't resist. "Buy now, pay later!" the sign stated. "Take advantage of our 12 months, 0% percent interest program!"

The salesman sold Gail on the $2,000 computer package with what appeared to be a great way to pay for a computer she could never otherwise afford. Gail wasn't worried. She'd put $600 down on the computer and decided she would put $140 aside each month to pay the computer off in ten months—with no interest!

Well, you know how the story goes...best laid plans. School started the next month, and Gail diligently put $140 aside for three consecutive months. Then, Christmas came, and she dipped into the fund just a little. *No problem,* she thought. *I'll just work a few extra shifts at spring break.* Well, that didn't happen; in fact, she lost her job and the saving promptly stopped.

Gail worried about how she'd pay the $1,400 bill when it came due but decided to deal with that when the time came. At least she had her new computer system to console her! In August, the bill Gail had been dreading came, and the news was worse than she'd feared. Gail didn't owe just $1,400 but $1,400 plus interest accrued over the entire twelve months.

*Those crooks,* Gail thought as she dug out her contract. *What happened to no interest for twelve months?*

Gail investigated and found the company had done nothing technically illegal. They'd even spelled out their terms clearly in the fine print Gail had chosen to gloss over in her rush to take her new computer home. It read, "The 0 percent interest only applies if you pay the balance before the end of the twelve-month term. If not, interest of 22 percent, compounding monthly, will be charged for the full twelve-month term."

Gail now faced a $1,708 bill for a $2,000 computer, even after paying the $600 down payment. And even worse, interest continued to be charged on that full amount every month. Gail could not afford to pay more than her original budget of $140 per month.

Best way to pay this off? If Gail wants to pay off this $1,708 bill in twelve months, she must make a payment of $159.86 each month (total amount paid: $1,918.32).

Since Gail cannot afford more than her original budget of $140 per month, it will take Gail fourteen months (just over a year) at $139.43 per month to pay off this debt (total amount paid: $1,952.02).

Gail ended up spending a whopping $2,552.02 for a $2,000 computer she didn't even need. Moral of the story: have a plan and a budget—and stick to it!

⌘ ⌘ ⌘

## ■ How Much Is that Dollar in the Window?

Do you know this one? Guy goes into an auto repair shop, he says, "There's something the matter with my car, it's making a funny ticking sound." The guy behind the counter says, "Leave it with us; we'll fix it for you, and you can pick it up tonight."

Would you ever take your car to the shop and agree to pay the bill without first getting an estimate? What about walking into a store and buying a large-screen television without knowing the price? Of course you wouldn't! Yet, most of us don't bother to consider the full price when spending our money—especially when using someone else's money (credit). Go figure.

You have to pay for the privilege of using someone else's money; you are paying for their risk to lend it to you. Every time you borrow money, you are using someone else's money. In fact, when you have money to invest, an alternative to stocks, bonds, and mutual funds is investing in mortgage and other lending funds. Those investors are earning the interest that you are charged.

Before accepting credit of any kind (including consumer loans, credit cards, mortgages, or lines of credit), you should be able to determine the true *total cost* of that borrowed money. You should be able to:

* calculate the total amount of money to be repaid (and therefore know the total cost to you for borrowing that money)
* calculate your monthly payment amount
* calculate how many months (and/or years) it will take to pay off the debt

This way, you can make an informed decision before legally binding yourself to something that could alter your future for a very long time—even forever. Let's look at the three types of costs related to borrowing: opportunity, fees, and interest.

## Opportunity Cost

"Opportunity cost" is a non-monetary value measurement. The *opportunity cost* of a decision you make is the value of the thing you can't do because of the thing you have chosen to do instead. For example, you may choose to continue with postsecondary education after completing high school. The future expectation is higher earning power and greater income. The opportunity cost is the wages you could have been making if you weren't going to school.

From the perspective of borrowing money, opportunity cost could include the amount of credit you no longer have available because you have used (maxed-out) your credit.

### Opportunity cost might not always be financial.

Way back in the introduction, I mentioned that humans tend to *approach pleasure* and *avoid pain*. While that seems like common sense, this concept can deeply impact our relationship and behaviour with money.

If you are tempted to spend money on something today (a new DVD player for example) and you take a moment to consider a future goal that you had in mind (let's say saving for a dishwasher to replace your broken one), the chance that you might decide to spend that money today is reduced significantly in order to avoid the expectation of future pain (the opportunity cost). If buying that DVD player today means you have to wait one or two months longer before you have enough money saved for the dishwasher, then the opportunity cost is the longer wait for the dishwasher—and the suffering from dishpan hands.

## Fees

Oh, they're there. Look for and question one-time fees that are sometimes charged by lenders. While it is not uncommon or unreasonable for lenders to charge an administration fee, these fees should be reasonable and not add a considerable amount to the loan.

Some fees you might see include set-up fees, administration fees, and even insurance (e.g., involuntary unemployment, disability).

Question any fees that are listed as voluntary. Many people are paying tens to hundreds of dollars every year for redundant or unnecessary insurance. That is because we are easily sold to buy insurance to meet financial commitments in case we lose our jobs or become sick or disabled. But you may already be paying for this insurance through credit card fees, banking fees, loan agreements, or even employment deductions. That means you are paying more than once for the duplicate coverage.

Don't get me wrong; insurance is *very important* (especially house, contents, life, auto, and unemployment). But there is no need to be paying for the same coverage twice. Make sure you check your credit card and personal loan statements for insurance premium notations. Credit card companies are notorious for up-selling their customers for loss-of-wages or disability insurance and identity theft protection policies. I have personally assisted people who gave in to a persistent telemarketer's sales pitches and later found out they had unknowingly agreed to a monthly insurance premium to be charged to their credit card. *You must take the time to find out what you are buying.* And yes, you can always cancel if you change your mind later. (Be sure to read the contract!)

Rule of thumb when it comes to a new debt: if you can't afford to pay the fees out-of-pocket at the time you are negotiating the loan, you need to seriously consider the risk of topping up the principal value of the loan to pay for those fees. Think about it: you are borrowing money to pay for borrowing money. The potential for this to become ugly debt is huge! The end cost for two loans at the same interest rate can be radically different when fees are factored in.

⌘ ⌘ ⌘

### *True Story: That's a Lot of Laundry Soap!*

Penny and Jake were in the market for a new washer and dryer. They agreed to use in-store credit. The sales manager went over the loan agreement with them, making sure to point out the 18.9 percent interest rate and the twenty-four-month term. He then reviewed the standard administration fee and the optional payment-protection insurance, carefully pointing out the burden this loan payment would have on the family if Jake were to become unable to earn an income. Concerned for the well-being of his family, Jake agreed to add on the payment protection insurance option.

Here are the terms of the loan:

| | |
|---|---|
| Original cost | $ 5,847.96 |
| Taxes (5%) | $ 292.40 |
| Total Purchase Price: | $ 6,140.36 |
| Plus 2.5% Admin Fee: | $ 153.51 |
| **Total Loan Principal** | **$ 6,293.87** |

*Without* the administration fee ($6,140.36):

| | |
|---|---|
| Monthly payment | $309.23 |
| Total paid | $7,421.52 |
| **Total cost of loan** | **$1,281.16** |

*With* the administration fee ($6,293.87):

| | |
|---|---|
| Monthly payment | $316.96 |
| Total paid | $7,607.04 |
| **Total cost of loan** | **$1,313.17** |

By including the administration fee in the principal loan amount, Penny and Jake paid an additional $32.01.

This lender charges a monthly premium for the payment protection insurance, calculated at 1.5 percent of the outstanding principal amount due each month. The first month (with $6,293.87 owing), the insurance premium is $91.12. The total amount charged over the term of the loan is $1,153.62.

The total cost of this loan with the interest, administration fee, and insurance = $2,498.80; that's $1,217.64 *more* than if they had paid cash for the administration fee and didn't need the insurance.

⌘ ⌘ ⌘

## Interest

Interest is what lenders charge borrowers to let them use their money. It is how they make their money. Up to 44 percent of a bank's income is earned through lending money; their *interest revenue* is the difference between what they receive (interest paid by the borrower) and what they pay to a saver. Banks also earn interest on their own investments and trading of securities.[32]

Interest paid is an expense to borrowers and revenue to lenders. It is very important to know how to calculate interest and to understand the terms that identify what type of interest you are committed to, because interest is a fee that you are agreeing to pay. Just like knowing the price of a car or a washing machine, you need to know the price of the interest you will be paying so you can make an informed decision.

### Dissecting Interest

Interest rates are always tied to a period of time that tells you how often interest will be calculated and charged. Generally, interest is discussed as an annual rate, but if the lender refers to another time period (*per diem* means per day), then you need to convert to what is known as the "effective annual rate." The effective annual rate is the *real* annual rate of interest. Once you know that, you can compare apples to apples (annual to annual).

### Two Kinds of Interest

There are two types of interest, simple and compound, and the difference between the two is significant.

*Simple Interest* is calculated on the amount owing at the designated time period. You can quickly calculate simple interest using the following formula: principle x rate x time = interest, or, **PRT=I.**

**P** (loan principal) x **R** (annual interest rate) x **T** (time period) = **I** (total interest)

Using that formula, let's calculate the amount of interest payable on a $5,000 loan charged at 18% over both a one-year and six-month term. Interest of 18% per year is equivalent to 18 ÷ 100 or 0.18.

**Time** (T) is calculated in years, so to determine this number (T) you need to divide the loan period—years, months, or days—by a full *one-year period* in the same value (1 *year*, 12 *months*, or 365 *days*).

**Here's how:** (multiply the underlined numbers)

**1-year loan**

P ($5,000) x Rate (18 % or 18/100 or .18) x T 1 (1 *year* ÷ 1 *year*) = **$900** interest payable

**6-month loan**

P ($5000) x Rate (.18) x T 0.5 (6 *months* ÷12 *months*) = **$450** interest payable

Simple interest is different from compound interest because the interest is charged only on the principal; interest that becomes due is not added in to that calculation amount.

**You do the math**—How much interest would you pay if you were to borrow $500 and have to pay it back in six months with 7% (annual) interest?*

Most all consumer credit (credit cards, personal loans, lines of credit) use compounding interest.

**Compound** means *a mixture or combination of two or more elements.* **Compound interest** means interest is charged on the principal and then added (combined) to the principal for a new total balance owing. The next time interest is charged, it is charged on the new total balance owing, *including the previous interest charges.* In effect, interest is charged on the previous interest charges.

---

* P = $500, R = 0.07, T = 0.5 (1/2 year). Therefore, I = 500 x 0.07 x 0.5; I = $17.50. You would have to pay back $517.50.

For example, when you buy a three-year loan with an annual compounding rate, interest is calculated at the end of year one and added to the principal still owing—as if you just added more principal to your loan. At the end of the second year, interest is again calculated on the total amount still owing, including all the principal (which includes any previous interest added in). The interest compounds (combines).

The formula for determining the total amount of compound interest isn't quite as simple as that for simple interest (pardon the pun!), but it isn't that tough either. To determine how much interest you will need to pay over the total loan, it is probably easiest to use an online calculator.

## I'm Just Saying!

Putting money into the purchase of a financial calculator may be the best investment you've ever made—saving you hundreds (or thousands!) of dollars. They are fairly easy to learn how to use: you typically need to know all but one the following inputs:

* Compound periods per year (1=annually; 12 = monthly; most credit cards are monthly)

* Interest rate

* Present value (what is the principal of the loan? Hint: it's a negative amount because you owe)

* Future value (of course, that's **zero!)**

* Number of payments for the entire loan period (typically twelve monthly payments x number of years)

* Payment amount

The one input you don't know is what you use the financial calculator to calculate! Handy, eh?

**You do the math**—Terry has a balance owing on his credit card of $1,395.00 which he would like to have paid off in six months. The interest rate is 18.9%. How much does Terry have to pay each month to pay the balance in full, with interest?

Use the following formula to calculate manually:

$$PV=PMT\left[\frac{1-(1+i)^{-n}}{i}\right]$$

Just kidding! Yah right. Okay, seriously. Use a calculator.

*Access online financial calculators at BrokeFreeForever.com.*

**Calculate using a financial calculator:** find payment [pmt]

* Present Value = ($1,395) *Because Terry owes this, it is a negative amount.
* Future Vale = $0;
* Interest = 18.9%;
* Number of payments = 6

Terry would need to make six payments of $245.58. The total payout = $1,473.48; total interest = $78.48.

Interest Period: To determine the amount of interest that will be payable for any one *interest period*, you need to find the *periodic interest rate*. This would be handy for determining the amount of interest to expect on the outstanding balance you owe on your credit card. To do this, divide the annual interest rate (R) by the number of compounding periods in a year (m). For the credit card above, the periodic interest rate is

$$i = R/m$$
$$i = 0.189 / 12$$
$$i = 0.01575 = 1.575\%$$

The monthly (period) interest charged is 1.575% x the principal of $1,395.00 = $21.97. If you want to work out the remaining monthly interest calculations on the decreasing balance owing, you can use an amortization table:

| Payment # | Amount Paid | Interest charged | Balance Owing |
|---|---|---|---|
| 0 | | | $ 1,395.00 |
| 1 | $ 245.58 | $ 21.97 | $ 1,171.39 |
| 2 | $ 245.58 | $ 18.45 | $ 944.26 |
| 3 | $ 245.58 | $ 14.87 | $ 713.55 |
| 4 | $ 245.58 | $ 11.24 | $ 479.21 |
| 5 | $ 245.58 | $ 7.55 | $ 241.18 |
| 6 | $ 244.98 | $ 3.80 | $ - |

There are over fifty-six million cards in circulation in Canada and one hundred-eighty million in the United States. The credit card business is highly competitive; there are more than 550 institutions issuing Visa, MasterCard, or American Express. More than forty card products have interest rates that are greater than 14.5 percent.[33]

Look over one of your own credit card statements to see if you can find the breakdown of the periodic interest rate charged monthly, as calculated from the annual interest rate charged. What is the periodic rate, and what is the annual rate?

### Beware the low-interest credit card!

Low-interest credit cards aren't always the great deal they appear to be. Many credit card companies will offer you an introductory low interest—but then increase the interest rate (sometimes substantially) when you transfer a balance from another card or after a certain period of time or when you use the credit for a cash advance. Suddenly, your 3.5 percent interest rate has grown to 27.9 percent!

Sometimes, the rules are very complex (tricky even). *You absolutely must read the fine print*; you are agreeing to all the terms offered when you sign the back of the card and begin to use it. Know what you have agreed to!

## ■ Comparing Options

Once you have figured out how to determine the actual cost of your loan, it is much easier to compare your options. Here are a few examples. Review these scenarios, and pick which option you would choose.

⌘ ⌘ ⌘

### Scenario 1

Which option results in gaining more value from a $1,000 annual bonus?

Option A: You can pay $1,000 towards a $2,762 balance owing on a credit card that charges 18% annual interest (compounding monthly);

Option B: You can pay $1,000 towards a line of credit (you have $5,400 owing and the bank charges you 7.5%);

Option C: You can spend the $1,000 on presents for your family and continue making your usual monthly payments towards the two loans; it is the holiday season after all!

Which option would you choose?

### Calculate the total cost of each option:

**Option A:** First, you need to compare the impact of the $1,000 payment towards what you would normally have otherwise paid. Let's say you are making payments of $120 per month towards this $2,762 credit card debt, and *you don't charge any more* to this credit card.

> $120 x 28.45 months
> Total paid    $3,414
> Total cost    <u>$ 652</u>

By making the lump $1,000 payment, you can pay off the remaining balance ($1,762 )in less time.

> $120 x 16.71 months
> Total paid    $2,005
> Total cost    <u>$243</u>

With Option A, you will save the difference of $409.
Add this to the value of your bonus for a *total value of $1,409.*

**Option B:** Again, you need to compare the impact of the $1,000 payment towards what you would normally have otherwise paid. Let's say you are making payments of $250 per month towards this $5,400 line of credit debt and *you don't borrow any more* from this line of credit.

$250 x 23.28 months
Total paid      $5,820
Total cost      $420

By making an extra $1,000 payment, you can pay off the new remaining balance in ($4,400) in less time.

$250 x 18.7 months
Total paid      $4,675
Total cost      $275

With Option B, you save the difference of $195.
Add this to the value of your bonus for a *total value of $1,195.*

**Option C:** By splurging the entire amount and not making any additional debt payments, the value is equal to what you gained ($1000) less the greater of what you could have saved (opportunity cost) by paying down one of your debts.

| | |
|---|---|
| Bonus | $1000 |
| Less opportunity cost | - $409 *(potential savings from Option A)* |
| Total value of bonus | $591 |

You gain the most by paying down the debt with the highest interest: Option A.

⌘ ⌘ ⌘

## Scenario 2

Your car insurance for a full year costs $1,875. You have the option of paying this expense over eleven months and paying an administration fee of $82 plus 3% (simple) interest. You have the

$1,875 saved up and could pay your insurance in full, or you could pay that amount towards your credit card with a $3,700 balance and a 21.5% annual interest rate. Currently you are paying $220 per month against the credit card. Which option will give you greater value for your $1,875?

Option A: Pay the insurance in full and continue making payments towards the credit card. Nothing changes—all habits stay the same.

Option B: Pay the insurance over the eleven months, and pay the full $1,875 towards the credit card debt (and continue making the $220/month payments on the remaining balance).

Which option would you choose?

## Calculate the total cost of each option:

**Option A:** First determine the total cost of the credit card debt ($3,700) with the existing payment plan. Since you aren't incurring any additional costs to the insurance, the cost of that credit card debt is the total cost of Option A, assuming *you don't charge any more* to this credit card

$220 x 20.19 months
Total paid     $4,442
Total cost     $ 742

**Option B:** Determine the cost of the credit card debt after applying the lump sum payment of $1,875. Then, calculate the cost of the monthly insurance payment option, since this is another cost. Then add the two costs together to determine total cost.

Credit card debt calculation:

$3,700 - $1,875 = $1,825

By making a $1,875 lump payment, you can pay off the new remaining balance in ($1,825) in less time.

$220 x 9.1 months
Total paid     $2,002
Total cost     $ 177

Now add the costs of the monthly insurance payment option:

| | |
|---|---|
| Administration fee | $ 82 |
| Interest | $ 59 |
| Total Cost | $ 141 |

The total cost of Option B is $177 + $141 = $318.

Option B costs you $424 less than Option A over the long term, giving you the greater value.

⌘ ⌘ ⌘

## Flashback

Remember opportunity cost? You need to consider the additional opportunity benefit to paying down the higher interest debt. That is, your credit card debt is paid off months earlier (in both scenarios). You gain the additional benefit of having a greater cash flow by eliminating that monthly debt payment a whole lot earlier. Now *that's* something to think about!

## Payback

Another factor to consider when weighing your borrowing options is to consider the payback period. The payback period is the amount of time it will take you to pay back the debt. This perspective is relevant when you are considering purchasing debt for the purpose of gaining an income or other future value.

⌘ ⌘ ⌘

### *True Story: Build It and They Will Come*

Donna and Mike wanted to increase their income. They already had their basement suite rented out to tenants, and the income was a huge mortgage helper. They had spent wildly over the past few years; every time the value of their home increased, they were able to consolidate their loans, and this gave them the opportunity to keep spending! Now that the housing market had stabilized, they ran out of equity value and could no longer borrow against their home to pay off their debts.

Now they were considering building a carriage house in their backyard. They could rent it out to earn more rental income. They still had untapped credit cards at Home Depot and Rona. Surely with the $10,000 available on their line of credit, the available total credit of $43,000 would be enough to build a simple and adequate carriage house. With a competitive rental market, they were certain they could rent it out for $1,200 per month!

If Mike and Donna were able to rent out the suite at $1,200 per month, let's calculate what the payback period would be if they spent $40,000 of their available credit to build it. To simplify this example, let's use a standard interest rate of 15 percent for all three sources of credit (Rona, Home Depot, and the line of credit).

To determine the payback, we will assume the total rental income ($1,200) is the monthly payment towards the debt. At a 15 percent annual compounding interest rate, it would take Mike and Donna forty-four months (that's just under four years) to pay back the $40,000 debt. And until they pay that back, they aren't realizing *any* profit; all of the rental income is going to pay back the debt!

Plus, Mike and Donna would need to increase their property insurance and absorb the cost of advertising and screening tenants, plus cleaning up in between tenants (time and money!). There were many smaller costs that may need to be taken care of in that four-year period—and their credit was tapped! They didn't have much breathing room left.

Mike and Donna decided it wasn't worth the hassle. Instead, they chose to upgrade their basement suite when the current tenants moved out and increased the monthly rent. They paid off the $4,000 upgrade with the incremental rental income ($200 per month) for twenty months—just under two years.

⌘ ⌘ ⌘

Mike and Donna's decision may not be the same as what you would choose; every situation is different. The important thing is to consider the long-term affect of your debt decisions. Here's another example.

⌘ ⌘ ⌘

### True Story: Retail Therapy

Cheryl loved her quaint aesthetics salon. She was busy with a steady and loyal clientele. While her service income was good, her retail sales were dismal. The layout of the salon was not good for encouraging product sales. Cheryl considered how she might like to renovate the salon to change the layout.

One of Cheryl's clients was a decorator. While having a manicure, the decorator spoke enthusiastically about all the wonderful changes Cheryl could make. Moving the pedi-stations to the opposite wall, having a new reception desk built, installing new light fixtures and mirrors—the ideas were fabulous! With a budget of between $10,000 and $15,000, Cheryl's head was spinning with great ideas of how she could make the salon beautiful and practical.

Cheryl's next client was a business advisor. As Cheryl shared the decorator's ideas, the advisor asked Cheryl how much she thought she might be able to increase her monthly product revenues with those renovations. After the cost of product was deducted, Cheryl considered her net profit from product sales would average to $1,000 per month, but she could expect a $500 increase immediately.

They did the calculation using a 10 percent interest rate. At $500 profit per month to contribute to the payback of the debt, it would take twenty-one months (almost two years) before Cheryl realized real profits that she could keep. And, until she was actually realizing the $500 in profit contributions, Cheryl would have to cover that debt payment from her service income.

Cheryl went ahead with the renovations, but they were scaled back to fit within a $5,000 budget. Her monthly profits *did* increase to over $500 per month, but it took seven months to get there. In this case, retail was the best therapy!

⌘ ⌘ ⌘

*Calculate the minimum payment amount needed to pay off a debt within a desired time frame using one of the payment calculators at BrokeFreeForever.com.*

# ■ Analyze Your Debt

### Taking a Debt Audit

It is fairly easy to calculate what your debt is costing you. Start by collecting the data on every debt that you own—the interest rate, compounding frequency, and term of loan, from monthly statements or the original loan documents. You can download a debt audit worksheet from BrokeFreeForever.com.

Step 1: List all of your credit cards, lines of credit, and loans in the first column of your debt audit worksheet.

Step 2: Determine the interest details of your debt.

The interest charged by credit card companies ranges drastically. Remember though, that annual interest most likely is calculated and compounded monthly using the periodic interest rate.

Banks and credit unions typically charge less for loans (you can check for up-to-date interest rates online), but reserve their best rates for those with a good credit risk. (Be sure to read the "Flirting with Your Banker" module to learn how you can increase your attractiveness to a potential lender.)

Look up the interest rate for each of your debts and record it in the debt audit worksheet.

Step 3: Calculate the total amount paid at the end of the term.

The total price of any debt is the difference between the total amount paid (number of payments multiplied by the payment amount) and the original amount (principal) borrowed.

To determine the total cost of the loan, multiply the total payment amount by the total number of payments and then deduct the principal amount borrowed.

If you do not have a set payment amount (such as when paying off a credit card balance), first determine what the monthly payment amount should be to pay off the debt in a desired time frame.

For example, if you want to pay off a $4,700 credit card debt in two years, use a financial calculator to determine the required monthly payment. Using my financial calculator, I determined that with a 17.9% interest rate, I would need to pay $234.42 per month to pay that debt off in twenty-four months (two years). I used these inputs:

* Interest rate = 17.9%
* Present value = ($4,700)
* Future value = $ 0
* Number of payments for the total loan period = 24

Calculate the total cost of each of your own debts **using the debt** audit worksheet from BrokeFreeForever.com. You might want to review the "Compounding Interest" section of this module.

Step 4: Categorize all of your current debt.

Which debt is reasonable, arguably quite costly, or might put you into serious financial jeopardy? Categorize your current debt into either good, bad, or ugly debt.

What is your most expensive debt?

Where or how can you decrease or eliminate the cost of your debt?

## ■ Help! I'm Drowning in Debt!

The second annual National Payroll Week Employee Survey found that *81 percent of employees* said that if they were to win one million dollars from a lottery, their first priority would be to pay off debt.[34] And, as interest rates threaten to rise, debt loads will increase both north and south of the border (Canada and the United States).

If you are feeling like your debt is out of control, you are receiving harassing phone calls from businesses you owe money to, or you are unable to meet your basic living necessities (food, shelter, utilities), then you will probably benefit from talking to a professional.

### Collection Agencies

If you are receiving calls from a collection agency, then someone you owe money to has submitted your file for collection. There are specific rules as to how collection agencies must conduct themselves. In Canada, visit the Industry Canada Web site for specific rules by province/territory; in the United States, visit the Federal Trade Commission Web site (Web site addresses are in the resources section).

## Seeking Professional Help

If you are currently not fulfilling your debt and bill obligations between paydays, you might need help to create a manageable plan to control your spending and debt obligations within your means. And that may include credit counselling and/or debt management.

What's the difference? Credit counselling is the activity of learning from a professional advisor about your personal finances and how to manage credit. Debt management is a program that you undertake to manage (and repay) your out-of-control debt obligations. There has been much controversy in Canada and the United States with regard to debt managers: there is very little regulation and few training requirements within the industry.

Solutions can range from an informal proposal to creditors (debt restructuring) that will help you focus on rebuilding your credit to formal (court process) procedures.

There are many options available to you; all you need to do is *choose to get help* and relieve the pressure. *But be careful!* Training, certification, and fee structures range drastically, and there is little regulation governing many of the service providers! I spoke with one debt manager who revealed that they charge over $700 just to help their clients create a budget—and that doesn't include the fees they charge to negotiate the debt restructuring. (Oh, and by the way, that particular "debt manager" did not hold any industry-regulated certification or accreditation.)

## An Industry Overview

Personal financial counselling is a wide field of practice that varies greatly in service offerings, certification, training, and governance requirements in both Canada and the United States. The most highly regulated end of the spectrum includes federally regulated financial institutions that serve consumers, such as banks; federally incorporated or registered insurance, trust, and loan companies; and retail associations. These institutions are monitored and supervised by, in Canada, the Financial Consumer Agency of Canada, and in the United States, by the Federal Trade Commission.

There is little to no governance or education requirements for individuals professing to offer credit, debt, and/or budget counselling and management services; most governance and education is voluntary and varied. Debt management and budget counselling financial services fall within the extreme wild-west end of the spectrum of the personal financial services industry. Really. Check credentials and references!

Individuals licensed to sell insurance and investment solutions obtain training via a number of accredited institutions and will hold credentials that emphasize managing investments or underwriting. Many investment counsel or portfolio managers will hold or be in the process of earning a certified financial planner (CFP) designation. All professionals with a certified financial planner designation receive their certification via the Financial Planners Standards Council (FPSC), a nonprofit organization that enforces standards for financial planning professionalism around the globe. As of the time this book went to print, the FPSC Web site indicated twenty-three member countries.

Other governed professional training includes the Insolvency Counsellors Qualification Course (ICQC) in Canada, which is the prerequisite course towards achieving the designation of a registered insolvency counsellor (RIC). The RIC is a designation required under the Bankruptcy and Insolvency Act for any individual who counsels debtors or offers credit counselling services in a trustee's office.

The Association for Financial Counselling and Planning Education (AFCPE) is a nonprofit, professional organization focused on education, training, and certification of financial counsellors and educators through their Accredited Financial Counselor program. This program is available in Canada via exclusive license to the Ontario Association of Credit Counselling Services (OACCS), and in the United States via the AFCPE directly.

There are thousands of organizations within Canada and the United States offering debt and credit counselling, debt management, debt relief, and budget counselling programs. The Federal Trade Commission provides a list of approved credit counselling agencies and approved personal financial management instructional course providers in the United States.

# ■ Summary of Module 5

This module focused on the three types of debt and three costs to debt. In this module, you learned everything you need to be able to calculate the cost of your debt and make informed decisions. After conducting your own personal debt audit, you will be able to analyze your existing debt and make choices about future debt obligations.

## Money-Boosting Strategies from Module 5:

Strategy #15:  Conduct a personal debt audit.
Strategy #16:  Know how much your debt is costing you.
Strategy #17:  Pay down your most expensive debt first.

## Access these Module 5 exercises and resources at BrokeFreeForever.com:

Debt Audit
Amortization Payment Calculators
Financial Calculators
Pamela's Industry Research Report
Reflection Questions

# Module 6:
## Flirting With Your Banker

*The surest way to establish your credit is to work yourself into the position of not needing any.*

—Maurice Switzer

## ■ What Are They Saying about You?

Credit bureaus track your credit and payment habits and provide it to companies authorized to access the information (including cell phone providers, department stores, and financial institutions). Your credit reports contain detailed information about your income and payment history, which is used to determine how likely you are to pay back a debt. If you don't pay your bills on time or default on a loan, it will be reported to the credit bureau and included in your credit report. Mistakes do occur, so it's important to review your credit report regularly and correct any misinformation.

You have the right to see the information contained within your credit report, and can get a copy for free if you are willing to wait for the report to be mailed to you.

*Direct links to the credit reporting Web sites are available through the BrokeFreeForever.com readers' site.*

## In Canada

Refer to the reporting agencies listed below to get the request form and instructions. For a fee, you can also retrieve your credit report online. For more information, contact one of the credit bureaus directly.

*Free Report via Equifax:*     www.equifax.ca

Look for the words "free credit file disclosure" and click on the link to open the printable form in a new window. You will need to send the completed form, with the appropriate copies of identification, to Equifax. They will then mail your free report.

The direct link to the form at the time of printing (may change) was:     http://www.equifax.com/ecm/canada/EFXCreditReport RequestForm.pdf

Contact Equifax directly:
1-800-465-7166
National Consumer Relations
P. O. Box 190, Station Jean-Talon
Montreal, Quebec H1S 2Z2

*Free Report via TransUnion:*     www.transunion.ca

Look for the words "free copy of your Consumer Disclosure" and click on the link to open a new window. The new page will provide you with instructions for ordering your free report via mail or in person at a Provincial office.

The direct link to this page at the time of printing (may change)     was:     http://www.transunion.ca/ca/personal/credit report/consumerdisclosure_en.page

The direct link to the form at the time of printing (may change) was:     http://www.transunion.ca/docs/personal/Consumer_Disclosure_Request_Form_en.pdf

Contact TransUnion directly:
1-800-663-9980 (prompt 1)
1-877-713-3393 in Quebec
Consumer Relations Department
P.O. Box 338, LCD1
Hamilton, ON L8L 7W2

## In the United States

You are entitled to a free copy of your credit score annually. You are also entitled to an additional free report if you've been denied credit or insurance, have had a change in credit limit, or other benefits within the last sixty calendar days, or you've recently placed a fraud alert on your credit file.

All US credit report requests are handled through www.annual-creditreport.com. You can download the printable mail-in request form from the Web site, and then mail it to:

Annual Credit Report Request Service
P.O. Box 105281
Atlanta, GA 30348-5281

The direct link to the form at the time of printing (may change) was: https://int.annualcreditreport.com/cra/requestformfinal.pdf

This link will start the download process to open or save the .pdf order form.

For a fee, you can also retrieve your credit report online. For more information, contact one of the credit bureaus directly. If you look hard enough, you can also find a link to request your free annual credit report through their Web sites. Where possible I have listed them here.

*Free Report via Equifax*　　　　*www.equifax.com/fcra/*

Contact Equifax directly:
1-800-685-1111
Equifax
P.O. Box 740256
Atlanta, Georgia 30374

**TransUnion**　　　www.transunion.com

Careful! The "free report" advertised on the home page of their Web site requires a credit card, and monthly charges of $14.95 if you do not cancel your *Credit Monitoring* subscription after the first "free" seven days.

After some searching I found the link to the free report by following this path: go to *Contact Us* then *Personal*, then scroll down to *Obtain a free, annual TransUnion Credit Report* and click on the link *download mail order form*.

The direct link to this page at the time of printing (may change) was: http://annualcreditreport.transunion.com/tu/disclosure/disclosure.jsp?loc=1470

Contact TransUnion directly: 1-800- 888-4213 (free report)

Visit the Web site for additional phone numbers.

TransUnion
P.O. Box 6790
Fullerton, CA 92834

**Experian**      www.experian.com

As with TransUnion, the $1 Credit Report offer on the home page of their Web site requires a credit card, and you will be billed $14.95 per month after a free seven day period if you do not cancel your Triple Advantage membership you have just purchased.

I found the link to the free report under their link to the *FACT ACT – Obtain Your Free Annual Report*. This link went directly to the Annual Credit Report Request Service Web site above.

Contact Experian directly:
1-888-397-3742
Experian
P.O. Box 9554
Allen, Texas 75013

**Don't get hit!**

Many people believe that every time a potential creditor accesses your credit report, the "hit" (enquiry) is recorded and lowers your score. This is not necessarily true. Multiple *recent* enquiries or many repeated enquiries over a period of time could be a red flag to creditors, indicating you have been searching around for credit. A pattern of many enquiries may lead a potential creditor to consider you a poor risk, especially if those enquiries did not result in credit being granted. Exercise caution when giving permission for someone to check your credit score, and only when absolutely necessary.

The most important information a creditor gets from your report is the pattern of how you handle your credit that you have. Do you pay on time? Do you carry a balance on revolving/unsecured credit? How much credit do you already have available to you? The risk to a creditor is, even if you aren't using the available credit now, the potential is there for you to use up all your available credit and not be able to pay back the debt. You can have too much personal credit.

## ■ Beauty Is In the Eye of the Beholder

Every lender has its own formula for determining the creditworthiness of a potential client; however, most consider the following factors when deciding whom to lend to and at what rate. Many of these things take time to develop, so it's never too late or too soon to start.

### Relationship History

No, not your romantic relationships. How long have you held a bank account with this or another financial institution? In all relationships, it takes time to really get to know a person. Take the time to make an appointment and discuss your financial goals and banking needs with your account representative. Let them get to know you and learn that you are trustworthy and working hard. When it comes down to it, sometimes the only difference between a "Yes" and a "No" is how well the person making the decision knows and likes you.

### Past Payment History

Do you pay your bills on time, even if it's just the minimum payment? Pay something—anything—on bills you cannot pay in full. Communicate with your creditors, and ask for help to develop a payment plan. Missed payments will lower your credit score—even if it's "just" your phone bill. This one small step will go a long way to helping prevent negative entries on your credit file.

### Current Debts

How much do you owe and to whom? Your debt ratio—the percentage of your paycheque that goes to repaying debt—should be no more than 36 percent to 40 percent of your take-home pay (and that's at the extreme high end!). Your credit report will show a potential lender how much of your available credit is utilized. Just because you have access to it doesn't mean you should use it all up!

### Employment History

Longevity is a good sign. Maintain a stable employment history. Lenders prefer clients who are at jobs for six months or more. This shows they are less of a flight risk and have the income to pay their bills.

### Your Net Worth

Put simply, your net worth (also called equity) is the difference between the value of what you own and how much you owe. You build equity by acquiring items that have long-term value, such as real estate and financial investments. But be careful! Not all homes appreciate at the same rate; in fact, mobile and manufactured homes can actually decrease in value in some markets. Homes built on leased land also appreciate less quickly. Your vehicle is a source of equity although usually not an appreciating one. A new vehicle's value decreases at rocket speed; in fact, some experts say a new car depreciates 60 percent as soon as it's driven off the lot. That's why the purchase of a newer used vehicle is often a better investment.

### Carry Insurance

Having insurance can help to increase your attractiveness. By having insurance coverage on your belongings, you are acknowledging responsibility and ownership by protecting your assets. Stability (maintaining coverage) over time and not having any claims can result in your receiving discounts on the cost of insurance coverage.

## ■ Ways to Decrease the Cost of Borrowing

Borrowing money is a fact of life; however, there are ways to decrease the long-term cost of using someone else's money. You can decrease the cost of borrowing by becoming more attractive to lenders. Lenders typically desire low-risk clients; that way, they earn their income with less chance (risk) of loss. Here are some ideas:

### Shop for savings on interest rates.

Shop around to compare interest rates. You may be surprised to find you can save as much as a quarter to a full percentage point, which can add up over time. Don't want to switch to the bank offering the lower rate? Ask your own bank to match the rate their competitor is offering. Many will.

### Compare credit card frills.

Not all credit cards are created equal. Consider all your options including cards that charge an annual fee but have lower interest rates (important if you carry a balance on your card). Remember, there is no interest cost if you pay your credit balance in full and on time every month. And don't forget to compare the rewards program (if applicable) for usefulness. How much is each point that you accumulate actually worth in dollars? Do you spend $1,000 to get enough points for a $50 blender? Are the points transferable to other people or rewards programs? Will you use the points? Is the program worth any extra annual fees that you need to pay?

### Have a cosigner.

A cosigner is someone with good credit who acts as a guarantor to a loan. The lender then has an additional party to go after if you default on your loan, making you less of a credit risk. Having a cosigner can help you establish your own good credit rating and secure interest rates lower than you'd qualify for on your own. It's important to remember that a cosigner is ultimately responsible for the debt if you default, so don't be late on even one payment.

### Monitor your credit report.

Follow up on any discrepancies that could affect your ability to qualify for credit. Look for errors and follow up to ensure they are corrected.

⌘ ⌘ ⌘

## ■ Summary of Module 6

Module 6 helps you to take a good hard look at your credit-worthiness, from the perspective of a lender. There are ways to increase your ability to secure credit, both in the short and the long term. Accessing and monitoring your credit rating will help you determine just how attractive you are in the eyes of your banker.

### Money-Boosting Strategies from Module 6:

Strategy #18: Monitor your credit rating on a regular basis.

Strategy #19: Know how you measure up in the eyes of a lender, and take the necessary steps to increase your attractiveness.

### Access these Module 6 exercises and resources at BrokeFreeForever.com:

Reflection Questions

# Module 7:
## Taking Inventory

*Life consists not in holding good cards, but in playing those you hold well.*

—Josh Billings

## ■ Why Budgets Don't Work

Over 60 percent of Canadians currently live from paycheque-to-paycheque,[35] and it is estimated this number is even higher in the United States. The question is: how do you break that cycle? When it comes to personal money management, the first thing most of us think of is creating a budget.

But while almost everyone has created a personal budget at some point, the majority of us are still finding their wallets empty before the next payday, even when their "income" column shows a bigger number than their "expense" column! Budgets have been proven to fail, over and over again, for the following three reasons.

### 1) Stuck in a Time Warp

Research has shown that budget estimates for one-year periods are usually more accurate than one-month budgets.[36] This is because most budget makers add a "room for error" amount when estimating expenses for a longer period of time (one year). Unforeseen expenses are psychologically easier to imagine over the distance of time. Most of us wouldn't dream of setting aside

$1,000 dollars for an emergency that could arise within the following month. We simply don't think that way. We tend to imagine disaster striking a little further from home, so a higher margin for unplanned expenses in the future agrees more with our self-protective psychology. Expense amounts over the long-term are usually estimated to be higher than initially thought.

When planning for a shorter term (one month), budget makers usually do not plan for the unexpected because they are *more confident* in guessing. They generally do not round up their estimates (probably because the money is harder to "spend" on paper), and the reality of actual spending is typically higher than estimated. When there is a small, or zero, margin for error, the budget doesn't work.

Small expense amounts not included in the budget add up to a significant enough sum to throw off the short-term budget. Most budgets with a one-month time frame are *underestimated* over the long-term—and they fail. As an example, consider birthday parties and other personal celebrations. How many friends' birthdays do you celebrate in a one-year period, and how much do you typically spend for each one? Most people do not have a "birthday celebration" line item in their monthly budget.

## 2) Failure to Monitor

Once a budget has been created, it is often quickly forgotten. We humans are creatures of habit, and checking in to compare our actual spending to our budget estimate is not a habit many people have. It isn't until the milk has run out and there are still days to go until payday that the stress starts to set in, and then we wonder, "Where did the money go?" Unfortunately, once *anxiety* kicks in, we tend to do things that set us further behind financially, like borrowing against our next paycheque, using credit to pay for consumables, or going into denial and spending recklessly. That's not monitoring; that's reacting.

## 3) Failure to Take Control

So you are closing in on payday with $20 left. Can you control yourself to make it last? There are numerous research studies that suggest that you probably can't. Marketing professionals can point to all kinds of research showing why you probably can't hold on to that last $20 (and most marketers are quite keen to relieve you of that $20!). One study shows that people will spend money they can't afford to spend simply to restore their sense of power or to enhance their perception of their social status, when they secretly feel vulnerable.[37]

Essentially, budgets fail because the act of creating a budget does not constitute a money management plan. But it is an essential tool and one piece of the overall puzzle to breaking the payday to payday cycle.

The simple act of creating a budget will not help you to get out of debt, manage your money, or save for something important. You need to have a budget that has been planned with both a short-term and a long-term perspective, a plan that creates a congruency between how money enters and exits your life, and you need personal accountability; that is, you need to be accountable to yourself. That's not a budget; that's a *Personal Accountability Money Management Plan*. (I like to call it the PAMM plan!)

## ■ How to Create Your Own PAMM Plan

### Know How You Rate

Do you know how your own household spending compares to your neighbours? Probably not. Most of us have been raised with a "never talk about money!" taboo. That means that we frequently don't really know if our spending habits are normal or on par with average.

### Resist the Urge

Most of the impulsive (and/or regrettable purchases) we make are due to our inability to resist temptation.[38] Consider what you learned about self-control and marshmallows back in module 1. While the degree of temptation and the degree of available self-control will vary, the first step towards resisting temptation is awareness. It helps to have some long-term goals in mind and a system to remind yourself of those goals whenever you feel the urge to spend; when you feel "the money burning a hole in your pocket" as my grandma used to say!

## Track Your Numbers

The best way to overcome short-term estimation errors is to keep track. Track every penny that you spend, and you may be surprised at what you learn! You'll be surprised to find out how much cash travels through your pockets, or via your ATM card, for lunches, coffees to go, and other impulsive purchases. By the way, if you think "ATM" is an acronym for "always taking money"—you may have a problem! (See "Resist the Urge" point above!) This is why it was important to go through the tracking exercises we did in module 4. If you haven't done those yet, it's never too late to start!

By the way, there are many options for tracking your spending. Some credit cards now categorize purchases on the monthly statement according to where purchases were made (restaurants, transportation, hotels, entertainment, recreation, etc.). You can choose to use a software program to track all of your bills and spending and download your monthly bank statement transactions electronically for reconciliation. Today's technology makes it easier and easier to track where everything goes; it's just the matter of finding the system that works for you and then using it.

## Calculate your outgoing congruent with incoming frequency.

Expenses can be annual, monthly, weekly, or even daily, while most paydays are every second week or once or twice a month. Creating a short-term budget based on long-term expenses will give you the greatest likelihood to avoid budget failure.

But budgeting alone will not solve the payday problem. If you want to break free from living payday to payday, you have to eliminate the discrepancy between how money enters and exits your life. Use the "My PayDay Budget" system in the "Your Personal PayDay Plan" module to eliminate that disconnect and create a management plan that works with your payday frequency.

## Be accountable.

No matter how well you plan, you still have to be the one to carry out the plan. If you do not monitor, reflect, and adjust, you will not know why, where, or when your plan went off the rails.

Increase your chances of success by creating your *lifetime vision*, doing the *milestone goal* exercises in module 3, and applying the principles of transition from the "It Looks Good on Paper" module to set yourself up for success.

Most important, you must take the time to monitor your activity, reflect on your progress towards your milestone goals, and make any adjustments along the way as necessary.

## ■ Looking over the Fence

Knowing where you are compared to the average or the median is sometimes helpful, so you can see if you are "in the ballpark" to keeping up with the Joneses or if you are setting the benchmark for responsible money management. Ego and competitiveness can be healthy—especially if they assist your sense of motivation to increase your bottom-line net worth.

It is important to note that using statistical data is typically a long way from comparing apples to apples. Many factors will affect the reasonableness of comparing your expenses—such as *where* you live. For example, let's take a closer look at shelter.

### Example: Shelter

The Average Household Expenses chart (below) indicates that the average Canadian spends 19.2 percent of his or her income on shelter.

Of course, there are two sides to every average: low and high. On the high side, nearly 25 percent (approximately three million) of Canadians spend *more than 30 percent* of their income on shelter.[39] This higher figure is supported by the 2006 Survey of Household Spending, which suggests the highest percentage of shelter expense belongs to those in the lowest income group; they spend an equivalent 29.8 percent of their income on shelter.[40]

The annual spending survey data reports the lowest income earners spend an average $7,100 on shelter while the census data suggests an annual cost of $17,500 for mortgage holders and $8,480 for renters. Depending on where you live, these numbers could be quite accurate or way off.

## Apples or Oranges?

The following section includes statistics from both Canadian and U.S. sources. Beware! Due to collection methods, age (dates) of data, definition of groups (or categories), and currency differences, you cannot directly compare the data that follows. There are good sources of data available to you from provincial, state, and federal reporting agencies. Refer to the resources and references sections to do your own research and find data relevant to where you live.

### A Closer Look at Canadian Statistics

To establish some average baselines, let's take a look at some recent Statistics Canada data. For 2006, Statistics Canada[41] reports one half of Canadian households lived above and one half below the following median income levels (by household type):

| | |
|---|---|
| All households | $63,600 |
| Couple families | $70,400 |
| Lone-parent families | $33,000 |
| Persons not in census families* | $22,800 |

In comparison, the census data shows average *total expenses* for households *by type* are as follows:

| | |
|---|---|
| All households | $48,767 |
| Couples with children | $68,087 |
| Lone-parent (female) families | $41,574 |
| One person | $27,240 |
| Senior Couples | $37,150 |

The following chart shows a breakdown of the average household expenses[†] from the 2006 census data.[42]

---

* Non-family consists of one person living alone or two or more persons who are sharing a dwelling but do not constitute a family. Income is per person.

† The percentage indicates the proportion of total expenditures.

| | | |
|---|---:|---:|
| Food | $ 7,046 | 10.4% |
| Shelter | $12,986 | 19.2% |
| Household Operation | $ 3,251 | 4.8% |
| Household Furnishings & Equip | $ 2,131 | 3.1% |
| Clothing | $ 2,870 | 4.2% |
| Transportation | $ 9,240 | 13.6% |
| Healthcare | $ 1,867 | 2.8% |
| Personal Care | $ 1,158 | 1.7% |
| Recreation | $ 3,975 | 5.9% |
| Reading Materials | $ 264 | 0.4% |
| Education | $ 1,157 | 1.7% |
| Tobacco / smoking | $ 610 | 0.9% |
| Alcohol | $ 865 | 1.3% |
| Games of Chance | $ 260 | 0.4% |
| Misc. expenses | $ 1,087 | 1.6% |
| Sub-Total Expenditures | $48,767 | 72.0% |
| Personal Taxes | $13,634 | 20.0% |
| Personal Insurance & Pension payments | $ 3,832 | 5.7% |
| Gifts and Contributions | $ 1,505 | 2.2% |
| **Total Expenditures** | $67,738 | 99.9% |

Here is another perspective: average total expenses per household by *income groups*:

| Canada | Lowest Income Group | Second Lowest Income Group | Middle Income Group | Second Highest Income Group | Highest Income Group |
|---|---|---|---|---|---|
| Food | 15.6% | 13.9% | 11.8% | 10.2% | 8.0% |
| Shelter | 29.8% | 23.7% | 20.9% | 18.7% | 15.6% |
| Clothing | 4.2% | 4.4% | 4.1% | 4.2% | 4.2% |
| Transportation | 12.9% | 14.4% | 14.9% | 14.3% | 12.5% |
| Personal Taxes | 3.3% | 9.2% | 14.9% | 19.4% | 28.7% |
| Avg. Expenses | $ 23,780 | $ 38,510 | $ 57,353 | $ 81,227 | $ 137,820 |
| **Avg. Income** | **$ 24,719** | **$ 42,411** | **$ 67,394** | **$ 100,777** | **$ 193,295** |

## A Closer Look at United States Statistics

For 2007, the U.S. Census Bureau[43] reports one half of United States households lived above and one half below the following median income levels (by household type):

| | |
|---|---|
| All households | $50,233 |
| Family household | $62,359 |
| Non-family household (Male householder) | $36,767 |
| Non-family household (Female householder) | $24,294 |

The following chart shows a breakdown of the average 2007 consumer expenditures from the U.S. Bureau of Labor Statistics.[44]

| | | |
|---|---|---|
| Food | $ 6,133 | 11.6% |
| Housing | $10,023 | 18.9% |
| Household Operation | $ 5,099 | 9.6% |
| Household Furnishings & Equip | $ 1,797 | 3.4% |
| Apparel and services | $ 1,881 | 3.5% |
| Transportation | $ 8,758 | 16.5% |
| Healthcare | $ 2,853 | 5.4% |
| Personal Care | $ 588 | 1.1% |
| Entertainment | $ 2,698 | 5.1% |
| Reading | $ 118 | 0.2% |
| Education | $ 945 | 1.8% |
| Tobacco / smoking / alcohol | $ 780 | 1.5% |
| Misc. expenses | $ 808 | 1.5% |
| Sub-Total Expenditures | $42,481 | 80.0% |
| Personal Taxes | $ 2,233 | 4.2% |
| Personal Insurance & Pension payments | $ 5,336 | 10.1% |
| Gifts and Contributions | $ 3,019 | 5.7% |
| **Total Expenditures** | $ 53,069 | 99.9% |

How much does it cost for you to live, and how do your expenses compare to the national average?

| | Spent Weekly | Spent Monthly | Spent Annually | % of Annual Income | |
|---|---|---|---|---|---|
| | (record the amount you spend weekly in each category) | (multiply weekly amount by 52 and divide by 12) | (multiply weekly amount by 52, or monthly amount by 12) | (divide annual expense total by annual income) | Look up the Average from the table above (by income) |
| Food | | | | | |
| Shelter | | | | | |
| Clothing | | | | | |
| Transportation | | | | | |
| Healthcare | | | | | |
| Recreation | | | | | |

# ■ Getting the Numbers Right

### Step 1: Think short-term and long-term.

You now know just how important it is to include both short-term and long-term spending in your budget. But even when your long-term expenses are considered, research has shown budget items are typically underestimated. When short-term financial decisions need to be made, usually our entertainment or grocery budgets are the first to be sacrificed, leaving us to feel resentful about not ever having enough money. This means you *must include your day-by-day, month-by-month, and year-by-year* outgoing monies.

You probably have a good sense by now of your day-by-day and month-by-month incoming and outgoing monies. Now you need to pull together all the information you have been gathering:

❋ Spending tracking worksheets from module 4—If you haven't used this already, print a copy and start now. You can begin with your budget right away and use the tracking form to check in and see how accurate your guesstimates are.

❋ Any (bank and credit) statements, bills, invoices, whatever you haven't yet included in your spending tracking exercises;

❋ Information from your Personal Financial Performance Ratios worksheet (later in this module);

❋ Any incoming or savings-related accounting, including pay stubs and investment or savings account statements;

❋ Anything else you can think of that's money related.

To help you with your long-term thinking, consider the following questions.

❋ Do you pay your car insurance monthly or annually? What about house or contents insurance?

❋ How much do you spend on holidays in the spring, summer, winter, or fall?

* How many friends do you buy birthday cards or presents for or go out for lunch or dinner with on their birthdays? How much do you spend each time on average?

* Does your spending on clothing remain constant throughout the year, or do you have seasons where you spend more on new suits, shoes, or jeans? What about winter boots or coats?

* Do you save for your annual ski pass or golf membership? How much do you spend on gas for your boat? Do you take an annual vacation or camping trip?

* How much do you spend on music or app downloads or on new technology? Do you spend online on a whim or is it planned?

* How much did you spend on entertainment last year, and was it planned for in a budget or from an allowance?

## Step 2: List *everything*.

Make a list of <u>every single item</u> that costs you money, including voluntary spending—*all outgoing monies*. The key here is to be as comprehensive, as inclusive, as possible. Any out-of-pocket expense that you leave out will mean that you haven't planned for it, and when the time comes, something, somewhere, will have to give.

Using all the information you gathered in step 1, think about your *weekly, monthly,* and *annual* spending (hint: think of each one at a time). Let your mind walk through each day of the week and think of the activities that you will do—and where and when you might put money out. For the budget purposes, you will calculate daily spending as a weekly total.

Record all that you can think of. Indicate whether the expense is weekly, monthly, or annual in the frequency column.

Review the category suggestions in the "A Closer Look at Outgoing" section of module 4 to jog your memory.

*Use the Outgoing Monies worksheet from BrokeFreeForever.com.*

### Step 3: Categorize red | yellow | green

Now consider each of those items on your outgoing worksheet by how voluntary they are. That is, is the expense a committed expense? Is it an automatic payment taken directly from your bank account? Is it set aside for future spending? Categorize each as *red, yellow, or green*. These categories will help you to *manage and control* your outgoing funds moving forward.

Committed: Red—This money is committed to repetitive and ongoing expenses, such as rent or mortgage, utilities, and loan payments. This money is *not* available for spending.

Savings: Yellow—This money has been set aside for an upcoming annual expense or to spend on something you are saving for. You can dip into this account but tread carefully—if you spend this money on something other than what you intended, you may be suffering an opportunity cost or an unnecessary deficit down the road.

Spending: Green—This money has been allocated for spending on fluctuating and ongoing noncommitted expenses, such as groceries, clothing, entertainment, and personal care.

To make accountability easier, set up the back-end administration system of your PAMM plan. You can do this through your bank or by using jars, envelopes, or piggy banks—whatever works for you!

### Committed (red)

This typically works well as a chequing account. You can write cheques for your rent (that way, you always have a receipt) and set up automatic withdrawals for your mortgage and loan payments, utility bill payments, and other *recurring and ongoing* expenses. Once you register the expenses to come out of this account, you can determine exactly how much from every paycheque needs to be put into this account (using the My PayDay Budget) and you will always have these payments covered.

## Savings (yellow)

This also works well as a regular bank account—or subdivision of an existing bank account. Most banks offer no-fee savings accounts, where you only pay fees when you make a withdrawal. *See the note below about banking fees to discover how you can avoid multiple fees.* Many savings accounts pay minimal interest, so if you will be holding your savings in an account for a longer period of time (even six months or more), look into depositing your money into a guaranteed investment certificate (GIC) or other committed savings. Even if the interest is minor (1 or 2 percent), it's better than nothing!

## Spending (green)

This should be cash, a prepaid debit card, or the *only* account that your debit card is attached to. Once your allocated spending money is gone, it's gone! Until next payday, of course. If you are someone whose automated teller machine (ATM) card is confused with the always taking money card, then a *safer* option may be to use a prepaid debit card from your bank, Visa or MasterCard. A prepaid debit card is a reloadable card that you put money onto (just like a gift card from a store), and then every time you use it, the balance decreases by the amount you spent.

**Caution:** Make sure you understand the fee agreement on your debit card or spending account. You might be paying a fee every time you spend. Shop around; the banks are competing to get your business, so you can always ask for a fee structure that works in your favour.

*A note about banking fees:* Credit Unions are different from mainstream banks in that you must become a member, and as a member are entitled to receive profit-sharing dividends. Instead of an account number, you have a membership number, and their systems let you create one bank account (one monthly account fee) that you can divide (split) into categories—such as the three categories of the PAMM system—without paying multiple account fees.

Record all of the items from your Outgoing Monies worksheet into the appropriate category.

> Use the Red | Yellow | Green worksheet from
> BrokeFreeForever.com.

## Step 4: Create your personal budget.

Planning your budget is a great opportunity to make adjustments to your spending. Now that you have a better idea of your spending, expenses, cost of debt, and personal financial performance ratios, it's a good time to set your own personal limits—or make allowances—to incorporate what you believe is reasonable and fits within your income (living within your means).

Determine spending proportion goals (budget) that are right for you and your personal circumstance. The budget is used strictly as a measuring tool. By having a budget, you can determine if you are able to stay in control (and if not, figure out why not), and it can help you see at a glance where your money is going.

The Credit Counselling Society suggests the following guideline for an after-tax budget[45]:

| | |
|---|---|
| Housing | 35% |
| Utilities | 5% |
| Food | 10–20% |
| Transportation | 15–20% |
| Clothing | 3–5% |
| Medical | 3% |
| Savings | 5–10% |
| Personal & Discretionary | 5–10% |
| Debt payments | 5–15%* |

The My PayDay Budget provides for six budget categories: necessities, expenses, debt repayment, play and fun, savings for expenses, and savings for spending. These categories are also used in the My PayDay Budget summary printout.

---

* Refer to the Personal Financial Performance Metrics; a debt ratio of 40 percent or more is considered high risk. Try to keep your debt ratio below 30 percent. Even lower is better! You might refer back to the average household spending data in the "Looking over the Fence" section of this module and adjust as necessary for your personal situation and location.

Essentials—This category includes basics like shelter, food, and basic clothing. It may also include prescriptions if you have chronic health problems. Your phone, health care, and utilities could also be considered as necessities, though you probably wouldn't drop dead without your cell phone!

Nonessentials—This would include other voluntary spending, such as cable, Internet, subscriptions, transportation, and repairs and maintenance, for example.

Debt Repayment—Pretty obvious! Don't forget to include private debts, such as promissory notes and IOU's to family. (Don't forget your aunt Gertrude!)

Play & Fun—Make sure you allocate some money so you can live for today (while being responsible towards tomorrow). This might include movies, hanging out, going out to eat, and pocket money.

Savings for Expenses—This might include winter tires and regular oil changes for your car, your annual house or contents insurance, RRSP contribution, or other expenses that occur less often than monthly.

Annual Savings for Spending—This is where you can put money aside for items that you don't want to use credit for. Save up for that annual vacation trip, your new couch or television, or even gifts for special holidays.

Record your own desired budget proportions here. This isn't set in stone; they are likely to change over time.

— Essentials
— Nonessentials
— Debt
— Play & Fun
— Savings for Expenses
— Savings for Spending

## ■ Personal Financial Performance Metrics

A metric is a standard used for measuring or quantifying. Metrics serve as benchmarks; they allow us to compare our current financial position to our desired financial position and measure change over time. Metrics are good tools for measuring personal financial performance because they allow us to translate dollar values into a percentage or ratio, eliminating the distraction of actual numbers.

For example, you might think that someone earning over $85,000 has a higher net worth than someone earning less than $45,000. In reality, income doesn't determine net worth. If the person earning over $85,000 has high levels of debt and committed expenses, they might have a lower net worth than the person earning less than $45,000 but carrying less debt and fewer expenses.

Use the following Personal Financial Performance Ratios (PFPRs) to measure and monitor your own personal household financial performance.

| PFPR | What it is | How to calculate | Metric |
|---|---|---|---|
| Cut and Run Ratio | Measures your ability to eliminate all immediate debt obligations by converting any **immediately** available assets into cash. Include anything you could convert to cash in the next 48 hours. | 1. Total all cash available after cashing in, selling those things you can, and collecting any money owed to you. 2. Divide that number by the total of your immediately due debt obligations. | **1 and over is desirable.** Less than 1 means you don't have enough immediate cash to pay off your debt; greater than one means you have something left over. |
| Freedom Ratio | Measures the degree of freedom between your total debt load and your total assets. Similar to the Cut and Run ratio, but assuming you have more time (months instead of days) to cash in and/or sell everything you could possibly sell. | 1. Total all cash available after cashing in accounts and investments, selling everything of value, and collecting any money owed to you. 2. Divide the number from above by the total of all debt obligations. | **Any number over 1 is desirable.** 1.0 means you have a zero net worth: your debt and assets are equal. Any number greater than 1 indicates the multiple of how much more value your assets are worth over your debt. |

| Handcuff Margin Variations include: **debt load** or **debt service ratio** (using disposable income) or **debt to income** (using gross income) | Measures the proportion of breathing space between debt and income. *Most financial institutions use disposable income (after necessary expenses, such as housing, utilities and groceries). Debt to Income can be measured using gross income. | 1. Total all debt <u>payments</u> for a specific time frame (eg. Monthly). 2. Divide that number by your disposable income for the same time period. 3. Multiply by 100 to get a percentage. | **The lower the better. Less than 30% is most desirable.** Greater than 40% is considered dangerous or high risk by financial industry. The lower your handcuff margin, the greater your potential seed money for growing your wealth. |
|---|---|---|---|

For comparison sake: the following table shows the proportion of Canadian households with a Debt Service Ratio higher than 40% in 2007:[46]

| Income | up to $ 20,000 | 5.6% |
|---|---|---|
| Income | up to $ 37,138 | 3.95% |
| Income | up to $ 57,481 | 3.76% |
| Income | up to $ 85,000 | 1.74% |
| Income | up to $132,036 | 1.60% |

In the United States, the Federal Reserve Board[47] estimates average debt service ratios of 12% to 13% in the last decade; an increase from 10% to 12% over the previous decade.

| Breathing Room Ratio | Measures the zone of breathing space between income and expenses /debt. | 1. Total Income for set time period. 2. Divide above by total expenses and debt obligations (payments) for same time period. | **1 and over is desirable.** Less than 1 indicates a potential payday deficit. The greater your Breathing Room Ratio the better able you are to respond to emergencies, unplanned expenses and/or take advantage of surprise opportunities. |
|---|---|---|---|

| | | | |
|---|---|---|---|
| Prosperity Potential Margin | Measures margin between earnings and spending. This margin indicates your prosperity potential; the potential value of spending less than you earn. | 1. Subtract all expenses and debt payments from income (any time period). 2. Divide above number by income (same number used above). 3. Multiply by 100 to get a percentage. | **The higher the better.** The higher this margin the greater possibility you have to grow your net worth. Aim for an increasing positive number. |
| Debt Burden | Measures the additional expense your debt obligations cost you by way of interest expense. As interest rates climb, so does your debt burden. Increasing interest rates can become the tipping point to turn Bad debt into an Ugly debt scenario. | 1. Determine total interest expense on all debt for set time period (eg. Monthly). 2. Divide that number by your total income for the same time period. | **The lower the better.** The Canadian average has been creeping from 10% to 12 – 15%. |
| Leverage Hurdle Ratio a.k.a. debt-to-net worth ratio | Measures percentage of total debt against total assets. The greater the ratio, the less leverage ability of equity-holding assets. | 1. Determine total debt obligation. 2. Divide that number by fair market value of assets **less** total debt obligation. | **The lower the better.** Peaked at 23.7% (2008) up from 18.5% 1000-2006 |
| Constraint Ratio a.k.a. debt-to-assets ratio | Measures percentage of assets owned by creditors. | 1. Determine total debt obligation. 2. Divide that number by fair market value of assets. | **The lower the better.** Reached 19.0% (2008 – up from 15.4% 200-2006) |

*Download a blank PFPR spreadsheet from BrokeFreeForever. com. The spreadsheet will auto-calculate your ratios for you.*

# ■ Summary of Module 7

Taking stock includes identifying and acknowledging the details of your own incoming and outgoing monies, as well as considering that information from an external perspective. How does your actual incoming and outgoing measure up to other Canadians or Americans (average and/or median).

The more information you have about your own incoming and outgoing monies, and those of others, the better equipped you are to analyze your situation and make decisions.

## Money-Boosting Strategies from Module 7:

Strategy #20: Take stock of your incoming and outgoing monies, for both the short and long term.

Strategy #21: Have a personal accountability money management (PAMM) plan.

Strategy #22: Measure and monitor your personal financial performance metrics.

## Access these Module 7 exercises and resources at BrokeFreeForever.com:

Outgoing Monies
Red | Yellow | Green
Personal Financial Performance Ratios
PPFR Calculation spreadsheet
Personal Expense Ledger
Reflection Questions

# Module 8:
## Your PAMM PayDay Plan

*There are no shortcuts to any place worth going*
—Beverly Sills

## ■ Fixing the Disconnect

One of the greatest challenges to managing money is the disconnect between how money enters and exits your life. A payday plan that eliminates this disconnect will help you to eliminate the stress of running out of money before the next payday. My PayDay Budget will help you to match the frequency of your incoming with your outgoing, using the PAMM system outlined in the "Taking Inventory" module.

You can download My PayDay Budget spreadsheet application in both Open Source or Excel formats from BrokeFreeForever. com. There is a link to download Open Source Office if you do not use Microsoft Office's Excel application.

If you don't want to use a computer application, you can also follow the steps to do the calculations manually, using a calculator. Skip to the "Manual Calculation" section if you will not be using the My PayDay Budget spreadsheet application.

You will use all of the information you have gathered or calculated in the previous modules to create your personal payday plan. You will need a list of all your spending, expenses, debt payments, and income sources and amounts. With the spreadsheet application you only need to input all your information once, though you may find the need to update the information once in a while, as things change.

> *Begin by downloading a copy of the My PayDay Budget spreadsheet application from the module 8 resources at BrokeFreeForever.com.*

## Getting Started with My PayDay Budget

When you open My PayDay Budget, you may be prompted (depending on your security settings in Excel) to enable or allow macros.*

Open the file, and save it to your computer so you can save your work. The following section is meant to guide you as you work through the spreadsheet.

There are five sections: Income, Savings, Debt, Spending, View Budget

## Step 1: Click on the *Income* button to begin.

The first step is to record your payday income. Select how often you are paid from the drop-down menu.

Then insert your *gross* pay amount in the *How Much* field.

Record the deductions taken off of your paycheque in the deductions fields.

**Option:** if you prefer, you can record your *net* pay in the *How Much* field and *not* record deductions in the individual fields. It is up to you.

## What if my deductions are different on each paycheque?

In that case, you can record your deductions as expenses in the *Spending* section (best) *or* record the average of your net paycheques (over three, four, or more pay periods) in the *How Much* field. **Use caution:** this option will work over the long term but in the short term could cause trouble; for example, if you are relying on

---

* If you are unable to enable macros, then use the worksheet tabs to move between worksheets instead of the buttons, and you will not be able to use the *clear all* functions.

distributing a paycheque of $1,206 and only receive $1,023, you may have to make some short-term adjustments to your budget.

**What if I have taken a pay advance and that amount will be deducted from my next paycheque?**

Technically, a pay advance is a loan. Record your usual pay amounts in the *Income* section, and record the pay advance as a personal loan in the *Debt* section (with the full amount owing as a payment).

If you prefer to not change your debt information, you can record this repayment as a deduction on the Income worksheet.

**What if I have other sources of income, such as child support, sales commissions, tax rebates, or credits?**

Record that income in the *Secondary Income* section. Also indicate the frequency that you receive that secondary income: weekly, every two weeks, twice a month, or monthly.

If you receive a secondary income less frequently, such as every other month (or every quarter for some tax rebates), then first calculate your payday budget *without* including the extra income to determine how much of each paycheque should go where. Then, add the secondary income into the *Income* section, and let the spreadsheet recalculate (click on the *View Budget* button).

During the months when you receive the extra income, use the budget distribution that includes this secondary income amount, and use the regular budget distribution for the months that don't include the secondary income.

### Create Your Budget

Next, input your desired budget proportions. This will not affect any of the payday calculations, but it will help you to monitor how on or off track you are by comparing your desired budget with your actual spending.

Refer back to the "Getting the Numbers Right" section in module 7 when considering your budget proportions.

The budget proportions in light grey represent a default budget; you can change any of the amounts in the white field as you desire.

Make sure your proportions add up to 100 percent! If you see "Budget does not equal 100%," then you'd best check your addition!

*Be sure to save your work as you go along.*

## Step 2: Click on the *Savings* button to continue.

There are two categories to savings: *Savings for Expenses* and *Savings for Spending.*

In the *Savings for Expenses* area, record any expenses that you pay on an annual basis, such as insurance, car maintenance, property taxes, house or contents insurance, etc.

The *Savings for Spending* area is where you can allocate any amount you want to save for a specific item.

Insert an appropriate description for each line item in the description field, the total amount needed in the "annual sum" field, and the number of months until you will spend the money.

The monthly savings contribution is calculated for you. The *Minimum Monthly Savings* field calculates how much you need to deposit into your savings accounts each month. These amounts will be automatically inserted into the appropriate fields within the *Spending* section.

Refer back to the work you did in the "Taking Stock" module to ensure you have included all the categories of annual spending relevant to you.

*Don't forget to save your work!*

## Step 3: Click on the *Loans* button to continue.

### Debts

You can choose one of three methods for recording your debt repayments. Once you decide which option you want to use, select that option (A, B, or C) from the drop-down menu near the top of the worksheet. The debt payments are considered to be monthly payments.

*Option A* allows you to calculate your monthly payment based on the principal, interest rate, and total number of monthly payments that you input. This is especially helpful for an unsecured debt that does not have a term commitment, such as a credit card or a loan from a friend or family member.

*Option B* is where you can record a reference name and a monthly payment amount for up to five debts, assuming you know how much your payments are. This option works well if you are making a set payment for each of your debts.

*Option C* allows you to record one total amount that you pay to all of your debts.

### What if I have more than five debt payments every month?

You can add all of your debt payments together and record that total payment in Option C. Alternatively, you can add similar debt categories together and use Option B. For example, you could call one debt reference "credit cards" and add your monthly amount for all credit cards as one payment amount.

Hint: Use Option A to calculate the monthly payment needed to pay off a credit card balance. Remember to put any little extra towards that debt with the highest interest first. This will save you money in the long run.

*Remember to save your work!*

### Step 4: Click on the Spending button to continue.

The spending worksheet provides areas for your monthly expenses and spending and your weekly expenses and spending. You actually budget for your pocket money! There are four areas in this worksheet.

Be sure to use the appropriate PAMM category: the red lines are where you record amounts that will come from your committed (red) account; the green lines are where you record amounts that will come from your spending (green) account; and the yellow lines are where you record amounts that will go into your savings (yellow) account.

*Monthly Spending* is where you record the descriptions and amounts of any monthly expenses and spending that you have. You can categorize your monthly spending under essentials and nonessentials to align with your intended budget monitoring.

The monthly contributions to your savings accounts is brought forward from the savings worksheet and included in this area.

*Weekly Spending* is where you record those daily amounts that you spend from your pocket. This might include transportation, entertainment, dining, and casual spending. Add up the daily spending for a weekly total.

The *Monthly Income Summary* keeps a running total of your spending to compare with your income. You will know when you are spending more than you have available because a huge amount of red warning text will appear. Adjust your monthly and/or weekly expenses accordingly until you have a positive *Remaining Funds* amount in the *Monthly Summary*.

The *Monthly Budget Thermometer* keeps a running total of your spending for each budget category. You can easily check to see how your spending compares with your budgeted proportions.

Start by inputting all of those committed and ongoing amounts, such as rent or mortgage, utilities, and telephone. Once you have input all of the committed amounts, then input all of the flexible or voluntary amounts. This makes it easier to adjust your voluntary and flexible amounts as you go if your spending exceeds your pay period income.

Be sure to refer back to your work in the "Taking Stock," module, and especially the "Getting the Numbers Right" section to make sure you don't leave anything out.

**Tips:**

* Set up all of your expenses that come from your committed (red) account to automatically be drawn from that account. You can do this by writing postdated cheques or setting up auto-withdrawals for those expenses.

* Make sure your ATM (always taking money) card can **only** access your spending account. This will help to avoid an impulsive and disastrous decision to tap into your committed or savings account at a later date.

* If you withdrawal cash for spending, make sure that you only take it from your spending account. When that money is gone...too bad! You have spent the allowable and budgeted amount and will have to wait until next payday. See the tip above to remind yourself that the money in your committed and savings accounts is already accounted for!

* If you tend to spend spontaneously, try this: put a piece of masking tape on your ATM (or credit) card with a note to think before you spend. That way, when you pull your card

out of your wallet, you will be reminded to think about what you are about to spend your money on!

* If you have and use a credit card, make sure that you only use the card when necessary and pay the total amount due when you receive your statement from the appropriate PAMM account. Think of your credit card as your ATM card, but the actual expenditure is just delayed coming out of your bank account. If carrying the card is too much temptation, put it in an envelope, seal it, and write a **note to self** on the envelope. Then put it away somewhere that is not easy to get to (like in a box buried deep in your closet or in a safety deposit box at the bank).

*Save your work again!*

### Step 5: Now you can view your work! Click on the *View Budget* button to continue.

This is the summary page of your PAMM PayDay Plan. It outlines your payday distribution, including a translation of all the income, spending, loans, and savings amounts from the previous worksheets. The *Deposit Summary* sets out the distribution of how much from each paycheque (or secondary income) needs to be deposited into the three bank accounts. You can even tear or cut off the top part to take to the bank with you!

The color-coded *Breakdown* indicates how much of that total deposit is allocated to each specific expense.

### Tips, Disclaimers, Caveats, and FYIs

Depending on how many cycles of paydays you have before your next committed payments are due when you begin using My PayDay Budget, you may need to make some minor adjustments to ensure you have a sufficient amount of money in your committed account.

For example, if you are paid twice a month and begin distributing your paycheque one pay period before your mortgage or rent is due, then you may not have sufficient funds deposited to cover that committed amount.

To overcome this, use the Quick & Dirty Paycheque worksheet (available at BrokeFreeForever.com) to determine the minimum amounts you need in your committed account for the next three to four pay periods. After you have cycled through one to two months of pay periods, you will have sufficient funds in each of the accounts to follow your PAMM Payday Plan.

Note: You will have a positive balance in your committed account. *Do not spend this money.* It is allocated to your committed obligations and needs to accumulate so that you will have the correct amount available when each commitment becomes due.

## ■ Creating Your PAMM Payday Plan Manually

Creating your personal payday plan will take a wee bit more time when you do it manually, but it isn't hard to do. You can download a blank PAMM Payday Plan worksheet from BrokeFree-Forever.com. Then, grab a pencil, some paper, and a calculator. (This won't hurt—I promise!)

Determine all of your daily, weekly, monthly, and annual expenses and spending (as above and/or in module 7). Write all of the items in columns to make your calculations easier, like the following example:

| Daily | Weekly | Monthly | Annual |
|---|---|---|---|
| Example 1 – 3.50 | Example 2 – 26.00 | Example 3 – 750.00 | Example 4 – 2600.00 |
| . . . | . . . | . . . | . . . |
| Total this column: $3.50 | Total this column: $26.00 | Total this column: $750.00 | Total this column: $2600.00 |

Then, add up each column, and multiply those totals by the number of those periods per year:

| x 365 days = 1,277.50 | x 52 weeks = $1352.00 | x 12 months = $9000.00 | x 1 year = $2600.00 |
|---|---|---|---|

Next, divide those totals by the number of pay periods you have in each year: (every week = 52; every 2 weeks = 26; twice a month = 24; monthly = 12) this example uses 26 – every 2 weeks

| ÷ 26 = $ 49.13 | ÷ 26 = $ 52.00 | ÷ 26 = $ 346.15 | ÷ 26 = $ 100 |
|---|---|---|---|

The total of all of those columns is what you are spending from every paycheque:

$49.13 + $52.00 + $346.15 + $100 = $547.28

To determine the PAMM account breakdown (Committed/Spending/Savings), repeat the above process but with three sub-columns for each frequency category. When you list each item under (for example) the weekly column, you will record the expense in the appropriate (Committed/Spending/Savings) subcolumn.

Here is an example of the "Weekly" and "Monthly" columns with totals:

| Weekly | Committed | Spending | Savings | Monthly | Committed | Spending | Savings |
|---|---|---|---|---|---|---|---|
| Saturday entertainment | | 50.00 | | rent | 750.00 | | |
| gas | | 20.00 | | groceries | | 375.00 | |
| produce & dairy | | 20.00 | | newspaper delivery | 18.75 | | |
| Doggie daycare | 25.00 | | | vacation savings) | | | 150.00 |
| Total each column | 25.00 | 90.00 | | | 768.75 | 375.00 | 150.00 |
| x 52 weeks = | 1300.00 | 4680.00 | 0.00 | x 12 months = | 9225.00 | 4500.00 | 1800.00 |
| ÷ 26 pay periods in the year | 50.00 | 180.00 | 0.00 | | 354.81 | 173.08 | 69.23 |

Paycheque contribution per account category for the above example:

Committed:     50.00 + 354.81 = 404.81
Spending:      180.00 + 173.08 = 353.08
Savings:       0.00 + 69.23 = 69.23

Voila! You now have a PAMM Payday Plan!

## ■ Summary of Module 8

In this module, you created your personal accountability money management (PAMM) payday plan using all of the information and data you have gathered or learned in the previous modules. Whether you use the My PayDay Budget application provided or choose to create your personal plan manually, this plan will serve as a basis to help you live within your means in the short term and accomplish your financial goals in the long term.

### Money-Boosting Strategies from Module 8:

Strategy #23: Eliminate the disconnect between how money enter and exists your life.

Strategy #24: Monitor your PAMM every payday; adjust as required.

### Access these Module 8 exercises and resources at BrokeFreeForever.com:

Personal Payday Plan
Quick & Dirty Paycheque
My PayDay Budget application
Link to download the Open Office application
Reflection Questions

# Module 9:
## It Looks Good on Paper

*Go confidently in the direction of your dreams! Live the life you've imagined.*

—Henry David Thoreau

## ■ A Closer Look at Transitions

You have a greater awareness of where you are (your point A) from your work in the previous modules, *and* you have a sense of where you want to go (point B) from your work in module 3 ("Onwards and Upwards"). You have also set out an action plan that correlates to your milestone goals.

But getting from A to B is a bit of a journey. Just because you have created a plan doesn't mean you will be successful in getting there. Change is a destination; the journey to achieve change is just that—a journey. It is a stage of transition from point A to point B, and you need to be aware of some of the challenges you will face along the way.

In his book *Managing Transitions: Making the Most of Change*,[48] William Bridges identifies the three phases of transition as:

1. Ending, Losing, Letting Go—letting go of old ways and old identities

2. The Neutral Zone—the "old" ways are gone, but the "new" may not yet be fully operational. This is a critical stage of psychological repatterning

3. The New Beginning—when new beginnings are made, new identities, experiences, and discoveries make the change begin to work

Bridges suggests transition is the process of unplugging from the old and plugging in to the new and that every transition "starts with an ending and finishes with a beginning."

## Step 1: The beginning is the end.

The beginning of your journey is the ending of old ways, the negative behaviours that are obstacles to your journey.

Endings may include behaviours or actions you identified in modules 1, 2 or 4, eliminating costly debt identified in module 5, increasing your attractiveness as a borrower as defined in module 6, or eliminating nonessential expenses identified in module 7.

Some of these habits or activities may be harder to change than others; the *degree of desire* you have to start ending the old ways correlates to the *degree of urgency* you have to accomplish the change! The more you want it, the harder you will work to make the change.

What old ways (thoughts, activities, and behaviours) do you need to end?

What is over? A chapter of life? A phase? What are you giving up?

What isn't over? What will you be gaining?

## Step 2: Stay committed.

The transition period is a time of redefining. It is a time of creating new systems (like the PAMM plan and My PayDay Budget). It may be a time of debt restructuring or creating new traditions.

Once you have established and adopted new money habits, you have to stay focused and dedicated to them! You will be tempted many times just this once to slip into an old behaviour, so you must be ready to overcome the craving!

It is very important to monitor, reflect on, and adjust your actions—as was set out in module 3, "Onwards and Upwards!" To cement the new behaviours, the new normal, into your conscious and subconscious awareness, it is also important to celebrate your successes, *all* of them, even the small ones!

Every small victory serves as reinforcement that you are on the right path, that you are making progress. Take a few minutes at the end of each day to think about your day. What goal did you achieve? What behaviour did you do or not do that serves to bring you closer to your goals? Give yourself a pat on the back for every action that you took that moved you towards your goals.

What new systems will you be adopting during this time of transition?

**Try This:** Choose some treats that you would like to reward yourself with while you are working towards your goal. These can be no-cost rewards or small treats that fit within your budget, of course! Write down your ideas for future reference.

### Step 3: Find your new normal

New beginnings will include all of the new habits, actions, and behaviours that you are intending to achieve. These actions will move you towards your goals.

This is where the personal *lifetime vision* and specific milestone goals (from module 3 "Onwards and Upwards!") help. Each milestone goal that you achieve takes you one step closer to your lifetime vision—just like rungs on a ladder. And, remember the mountain theory of goals—each step forward gives you a better view of other options and opportunities; your future keeps looking brighter and brighter!

Staying focused and dedicated will be easier with the support of friends, peers, or family. The transition process can be much easier when you and a friend are working towards a similar goal. It's never too late to start that peer group!

Identify those people whom you would like to have in your own Broke-Free Forever peer group.

⌘ ⌘ ⌘

### *True Story: Hamster Loan*

Jean was becoming frustrated with her nine-year-old son's constant pleas. Struggling to make ends meet on her administrative salary meant she couldn't just go out and buy Justin everything he wanted—even if "Everyone else has one!" Justin's latest desire was a hamster. He just didn't understand that the hamster came with a whole bunch of other ongoing costs, like the food and wood chips, in addition to the cost of the elaborate wheel cage! Jean needed to teach Justin some money accountability.

While Justin had already been receiving an allowance, Jean decided to bring it up a notch. Justin would receive a bigger allowance every payday, but he had to continue with his allotted chores and work as Jean's "assistant" every payday as she paid the bills and planned the grocery list.

In exchange, Jean would give Justin a loan for the hamster and all the associated goodies. Every payday, a payment towards the loan would be deducted from Justin's allowance. Justin agreed, and Jean gave him an old chequebook register to record the initial principal and subsequent payments. Then they went out and bought the hamster, complete with hamster castle and a month's worth of supplies.

About two weeks later, when Justin's first loan payment was due, he was not too happy that Mom was really going to deduct a $5.00 hamster loan payment. Reality was setting in; his pocket money was limited. Then Justin got to use the calculator and help Jean add up the bills due and deduct them from her paycheque. After many questions about the payroll deductions and why they had to pay for utilities, Justin saw how quickly the money ran out.

Justin soon learned to respect his earnings and took extra care to ensure the cage supplies weren't wasted. He also soon found it fun to try to find groceries priced lower than those his mom found when they went shopping!

⌘ ⌘ ⌘

## ■ Don't Become Complacent

Continuing in your current patterns will not get new results. But you must also be patient—ingraining new habits takes time! Staying motivated to achieve your goals is critical. In addition to having a support team, you can stay motivated by reminding yourself why you are doing what you are doing.

**Try this:** What motivates you to achieve your financial goals? Is it a future state of comfort or financial freedom? Is it living a stress-reduced life? Are your goal outcomes more promotion or prevention focused? Are you trying to achieve something positive or avoid something negative?

Review your lifetime and milestone goals and *why* these goals are important to you.

### Staying Motivated

Motivation is the intensity and persistence to achieve that desired goal or undertake that new behaviour or action. Possessing a strong positive intention or making a strong commitment is critical to achieving behavioural change.[49]

Stanley Thomas and William Danko (authors of *The Millionaire Next Door*) found out just how important persistence and motivation is when he was researching millionaires. Over seven hundred millionaires surveyed ranked two of the top five success factors for achieving personal economic success as "working harder than most people" and "being well disciplined."[50]

Motivation is a major component in the willingness to work hard and maintain self-discipline. The more motivated you are, the harder you are willing to work, and the more disciplined you will be in achieving your goals.

How motivated do you believe you are to achieve your financial goals?


What can you do to increase your motivation (sense of urgency) or remind yourself to stay motivated when faced with temptation?

## A Special Note to Couples and Families

When there are two or more of you involved in any kind of transition, you need to be prepared that both (or all) of you may not go through the stages at the same time or always share the same degree of motivation. Because of this, you may need to exercise more patience with each other and help each other by being supportive and open.

Because you are not going through this transition alone, you can act as each other's support system and (nicely) hold each other accountable. You are fortunate though, since change can be easier when you have someone to share the experience with.

Remember all that self-awareness work you did in modules 1 and 2? Consider the personality traits, belief systems, and perspectives of those you are going through this transition with. Consider how you can learn from each other and how each of you can achieve together, but with different methods, perspectives, and rewards. Just because someone isn't doing something the same way you are doesn't make his or her method or perspective wrong; it just makes it different. Be gracious, compassionate, and tolerant with each other.

## A Special Note to Individuals

Going through transition by yourself can be difficult without anyone to support you or hold you accountable. If you decide to do it alone, adopt some measures to stay accountable to yourself, like regular rewards and participating in the e-coaching support from BrokeFreeForever.com.

Or, find someone to go through this process with you! You must know *someone* who needs to get ahead financially! Find a friend or colleague who is keen to share in this program and commit to checking in with each other weekly.

You may even find it fun to form a peer group of three to six people and meet once a month to share tips, ideas, and progress reports on how you're doing. You can meet face-to-face or just check in with each other every week by e-mail.

Just remember that this is a personal journey for everyone, and anything that is shared must be kept confidential. And no judgements! Everyone should feel free to share his or her thoughts without receiving judgements or advice from his or her peer group. Should you choose to form a peer group, please read the note above to couples and families. Be gracious, compassionate, and tolerant with each other.

## With a Little Help from My Friends

Do you believe that you will be generally supported in your change process? Yes or No. Why?

Who do you think will support you? List the names of those you can share your goals with and receive support and encouragement from.

Who do you think might be averse to your succeeding in this change?

How might you develop your support circle to increase the support you receive?

## ■ Summary of Module 9

Achieving change is much more than knowing where you are starting from and where you intend to get to. A goal is the destination, but getting there takes attention to the change process. Some of the major obstacles to achieving change were addressed in this module.

**Money-Boosting Strategies from Module 9:**

Strategy #25: Be aware of which transition phase you are in.
Strategy #26: Don't become complacent.
Strategy #27: Have a support system.


**Access these Module 9 exercises and resources at BrokeFreeForever.com:**

*Think and Grow Rich* (public domain) by Napoleon Hill
Intention Cards
Reflection Questions

# Module 10:
# Rome Wasn't Built in a Day

*There are no secrets to success. It is the result of preparation, hard work, and learning from failure.*

—Colin Powell

## ■ Secrets to Financial Freedom

There really isn't any secret. Most people just don't want to accept the truth. Success takes some effort. Growing your money also takes seeds. Flashback to module 4, "Money 101": the money left over after deducting all the outgoing from the incoming represents the seeds of possibility.

This is because that money, the leftover, the discretionary income, the surplus—whatever you want to call it—is what you have for investing or saving, for now and your future. If you want to grow that money, you need to plant it (invest it) where there is opportunity for it to grow.

### You Reap What You Sow

Though it would be great to be reaping what we have sown during our younger years and most of us would like to stop working sooner than later, the reality is that for most of us, that time will probably be later rather than sooner. Whether your aim is sooner or later, you need to determine how much money you will need to live on at that time.

For retirement planning, most financial planners will recommend that you plan to live on 60 to 80 percent of your existing income to maintain a similar lifestyle. And, if you aren't earning that money, then your primary source of that incoming money will be from secondary sources (pensions, investments, royalties, etc.; review the "A Closer Look at Incoming" section of module 4).

The more seed money you have to grow, the more options you have and the greater probability for those secondary income sources to flourish.

### So how do you get more seeds?

Remember millionaire researchers Stanley and Danko? They shared some interesting findings about the millionaires they surveyed:

* they live on less than 7 percent of their total wealth; they **all** live well **below their means** (spend less than they receive)
* most have a **detailed, up-to-date budget**
* they all **save at least 15 percent of their earned income**
* they **invest nearly 20 percent** of household income every year
* 20 percent are **not** college graduates but believe education is extremely important
* 33 percent are self-employed, and
* Over 65 percent **work between forty-five and fifty-five** hours per week.

It takes time to reap what you sow, but the most important thing is to get to that place where you *have* some seeds to sow! That would be the money you have left over after paying your bills—and keeping your spending in check (incoming less outgoing = possibility).

Once you get started, tracking the growth of your financial wealth can be addictive! There is a net worth tracking spreadsheet available in online resources for module 9.

And you might be surprised with how little you need to get started. Sure, $20 a month may not be as powerful as the magic beans Jack got from selling his cow, but there are lots of things you can begin with that small of a contribution.

Now let's look at your incoming money from another perspective: active versus passive.

### The Passive Income Secret

*Active income* is that money you receive for trading your time (time spent doing some activity) or trading your stuff (selling goods). Another way to think of active income is that this source of income would most likely stop if you became sick, disabled, or died, or ran out of stuff.

**Review from "Money 101" module:** There are two limits on the income earned by exchanging time spent:

1. The limit on the number of hours per day that we can exchange—No matter if you are a taxi driver, waiter, baker, accountant, mechanic, nurse, lawyer, or assembly-line worker, there are only twenty-four hours in each day, and you have to spend some of those sleeping, eating, and washing up (among other things).

2. The market value of the money paid per hour—Depending on what activity, skill, or knowledge you are trading by the hour and where you might live, the value may be quite different.

*Passive income* is money that you earn that is *not* tied to an exchange for hours or an exchange for stuff. Think of it as money you earn while you sleep. This can include money earned from the sale of products (including royalties earned from music or other performing arts), dividends from stocks, and even interest on money invested (savings, bonds, or mutual funds). This money is passive because you are not actively trading something for it. Another way to think of passive income is that this source of income would not stop if you became sick, disabled, or died; it may continue to be paid to your estate or assigned to a third party.

Increasing the availability of passive income provides you with more seed money that isn't constrained by the time or inventory of goods that you have available to trade for income. One way of increasing your passive income is through investing.

## Investing 101

There are two cardinal rules to investing:

1. Buy low, sell high, and
2. Risk and return are negatively correlated.

### 1. Buy Low, Sell High

It sounds pretty simple, but you'd be surprised how difficult that can be! Much of investing is speculation—educated guessing. You need to do some research into the investment you are considering so you can make the determination of what "low" might reasonably be. Seek out and collect as much information as you can on the investment you are looking at, including its historical performance, professional and expert outlooks (industry and market), and relevant economic factors.

And leave your emotions out of it! Typically, when a stock is realizing a growth trend, investors are happy and giddy and eager to watch the rise. This may influence a decision to "buy more" of this investment—and that usually means you are buying at an inflated (high) price. Likewise, an investment experiencing a decrease in value might instigate feelings of panic and fear, and some may choose to "sell quickly" while the price is low.

To avoid this, do your homework and consider your investments over the long term. Markets have been going up and down for decades and are expected to continue those cycles!

If you want to learn more, attend one of the many investment workshops frequently hosted by local financial planners and investment firms. Or better yet, make an appointment with a financial planner to learn how he or she can help you. After all, financial planners have been trained and educated to provide advice. And they want to help you increase your net worth.

On that note, the following contributions are from some of my own colleagues who are financial advisors. They work with clients from all types of backgrounds and with varying levels of net worth. You don't need to be rich to have a financial advisor; find someone who is committed to helping you grow your wealth no matter what contribution you can make today.

Even with only $20 or $30 per month available, a financial planner can assist you to start growing that seed money right away. It's never too early—or too late—to begin.

⌘ ⌘ ⌘

### Second Opinion: Jery Urquhart, Sunlife Advisor

"A penny saved" is a crappy savings plan. In order to make a difference and provide a retirement that reflects your current lifestyle, one should be taking 20 percent of current earnings and purchase insurances as well as savings into a tax-free account and/or RRSP. Insurance plans can provide security now as well as accumulate savings for the future.

Using a percentage of earnings takes into account increasing incomes, lifestyle adjustments, and the effects of inflation. Starting today is important so the compound growth can start. Two important issues to remember are: small is better than zero, and a financial advisor pays huge dividends and costs little or nothing.

### Second Opinion: Lisa Jaffary, Points West Insurance

A financial advisor can help you develop a healthy money relationship. Your advisor is independent and helps you manage your money. He/she helps you create goals, teaches you how to save, and implements a system that works with you.

Plan to meet with two or three financial advisors. Ask them questions like what type of investments do they have access to—all investments or a limited number of funds? How often do they contact their clients? How do they get paid? Think about how comfortable you are with them. Do you feel listened to?

We need money to live, and earning an income is part of life. How you treat money and what you do with it makes the difference. By saving and investing a portion of your income, you can build your wealth with emergency money, holiday accounts, and retirement funds. Accounts such as RRSPs and TFSAs (tax-free savings accounts) are examples of where you can invest your money.

An example of a savings account is a "rainy day account." The new TFSA is an ideal account for this. First, put a purpose to this account. Would you like to save for a holiday? A big purchase item?

Or retirement? A purpose goes a long way to a healthy rainy day account.

By creating several different pots of money, you will have flexibility. During your working years and when you retire, you will have money to draw upon.

⌘ ⌘ ⌘

## Sir John Templeton

The late Sir John Templeton was a very successful businessman and investment guru and seemed to be well respected for his character. Templeton is well-known for this following list of rules for success.[51]

### Sixteen Rules for Investment Success
### (and for Your Family, House, Tuition, Retirement...)

By Sir John Templeton, Franklin Templeton Investments

1.  Invest for maximum total *real* return (return on invested dollars after taxes and inflation).
2.  Invest—Don't trade or speculate.
3.  Remain flexible and open-minded about types of investment.
4.  Buy low.
5.  When buying stocks, search for *bargains* among *quality* stocks.
6.  Buy value, not market trends or the economic outlook.
7.  Diversify—in stocks and bonds; as in much else, there is safety in numbers.
8.  Do your homework or hire wise experts to help you.
9.  Aggressively monitor your investments.
10. Don't panic.
11. Learn from your mistakes.
12. Begin with a prayer.
13. Outperforming the market is a difficult task.

14. An investor who has all the answers doesn't even under-stand all the questions.

15. There's no free lunch.

16. Do not be fearful or negative too often.

## ■ Protecting Your Ass-ets

You work so hard for so many years to acquire the fruits of your labour. Your big-screen television, the comfy pillow-top mat-tress, the functional yet pretty stoneware dishes, the microwave, the coffeemaker and margarita blender, the tools, the shoes, the camping gear...the list goes on.

Then disaster strikes. A candle was left burning overnight, the wiring on the space heater malfunctions, the renters upstairs (next door, downstairs) fail to extinguish a cigarette or lightning strikes (figuratively or literally), and poof!—It's gone, or at least damaged beyond recognition.

Take a few minutes to add up the *replacement value* of every item in every room of your home. Start by creating a list of belong-ings for *every room* in your house. Don't forget your storage shed!

It doesn't take much effort to find examples in the news of people losing all their material possessions due to fires, floods, and other weather-related and unforeseen disasters. And even more discouraging is when you read that a family has lost everything and they didn't have insurance.

How would you pay to replace all your necessities? If you own your home and have a mortgage, then you typically have to have home insurance (a condition of the mortgagor), and usually, that coverage includes content replacement and varying degrees of emergency shelter expense and even some personal liability.

But if you rent, then having insurance coverage is optional: that means it is *up to you—your option* to go and get it. The approxi-mate cost for tenant's content insurance for a twenty-three year old non-smoker living in various locations across Canada ranges from $195 to $360 per year.[52] If you have roommates, the cost may increase substantially as the risk is now greater for loss, and it may be very difficult to get. **Insider secret:** if your insurance agent turns you down for tenant's content coverage, talk to another agent. An agent probably knows of an underwriter that will give you coverage, but the underwriter wants an assurance from the agent that you are risk-worthy. Just like hairstylists and mechanics, it can be very convenient to have an insurance agent as a friend!

*Access the free online home inventory at BrokeFreeForever.com*

## ■ Protecting your income

What would happen if your primary source of income came to a halt? Consider what would happen if you were to become critically ill or disabled. Most of us know someone (through work, friends or family) who is dealing with a critical illness. And being sick isn't cheap. Many people have lost their homes while trying to stay alive and cover the cost of medication or treatments.

And if you are counting on the income protection that you are paying to your credit card company at the rate of $15 per month (or so), you'd best read the fine print. Don't have a copy of the policy? Well you'd better get one!

⌘ ⌘ ⌘

### *True Story: that's not what I paid for!*

Denise received a telephone call during dinner. "Hello, this is your credit card company calling and we have a special offer for you for loss of income coverage. This will only cost you $15 per month. May we sign you up?" After a short discussion with the agent, Denise decided this was a really good deal. She told the agent that she had a good medical plan through her employer, but did not have any loss of income coverage. "This will be good protection" she thought to herself. She made a notation on her credit card statement that read $15 per month – loss of income, and didn't think about it again.

For the next three years $15 per month was charged to her credit card. Then it happened. While playing softball Denise took a tumble running the bases and required surgery to her knee. The day after coming out of the hospital Denise called the credit card company to find out about her loss of income insurance. The customer service representative informed Denise: "I'm sorry, but you don't have loss of income insurance; you have a policy for extended medical benefits." "But I've been paying for that coverage for over three years!" she exclaimed. The agent disagreed. Denise was sick with worry and felt the blood drain from her face as she called her friend to share what had happened. Her friend asked her, "Well, don't you have a copy of the policy so you can dispute their claim of what you paid for?" Denise didn't. She hadn't noticed that she never received a copy of the policy – now it was her word against theirs.

⌘ ⌘ ⌘

Denise learned the hard way: without a copy of what she supposedly paid for, it was her word against the policy holder as to what coverage she had.

There are many options for obtaining income protection, and the options will vary in cost depending on how much you need. It doesn't cost any money (or shouldn't!) to consult with an accredited insurance agent to look into options. And, because each insurance agent may be limited with the insurance products they have available to sell to you, be sure to get a few opinions and meet with agents from a few different companies.

* **Mortgage Insurance**—is a life insurance policy that pays the balance of a mortgage if the insured dies.

* **Disability Insurance**—also known as disability income insurance, this insurance will provide the beneficiary an income should a disability make working (and therefore earning) impossible.

* **Long Term Care Coverage**—is designed to help you cover expenses in case of a non-life-threatening chronic illness, long-term disability, or otherwise become unable to live independently.

* **Critical Illness**—is intended to help financially support the beneficiary before, during and after treatment for a critical illness. It typically provides a lump-sum benefit when a critical illness is diagnosed.

## ■ Infinity and Beyond!

I always wonder when I hear someone saying, "If something happens to me..." There is no *if* about it. One day, you will leave this life. In fact, it's guaranteed.

If you fail to plan for when you *do* exit this life, it can be extraordinarily costly to those left behind—and even cause grief and anxiety when it does not need to.

This is where an estate planner comes in. Once you have built up your net worth, your estate, you need to make sure that it doesn't all go to the default government estate plan when you are through with this lifetime. And, if you haven't made your own estate plan, then guess what—the government will determine where your estate goes, and they don't do that for free.

Estate planning can include trust planning, tax shelter strategies, and even funeral planning.

If you want to learn more, attend one of the many estate planning workshops frequently hosted by local financial planners and estate planning firms. Or better yet, make an appointment with an estate planning professional to learn how he or she can help you. After all, these people have been trained and educated to provide advice. And they want to help you protect your net worth for you and future generations.

## ■ Happy Birthday to Me!

It can be overwhelming to think about the administration side of life. But taking some time to be proactive can save you many hours and lots of aggravation, stress, and *money* when (not if!) something happens.

Get into the habit of celebrating the anniversary of your existence (your birthday!) by reviewing your current and future income, your current net worth and insurance coverage, your estate planning, and your will. If you haven't already, consider preplanning your exit too.

Your birthday is not only a great time to review your financial and administrative status, it is also a great opportunity to take some time out for you, to consider your lifetime vision and milestone goals and review all the achievements, successes, and lessons from the past year.

# ■ Summary of Module 10

Unlike the many claims out there of ways to "get rich quick," the tried-and-true route to personal financial freedom takes time. Module 10 addresses how to grow your income and assets: important factors to offsetting your personal debt and growing your personal net worth. Once you have a positive net worth, you will want to consider how you would like to best protect and eventually disburse your estate in the way that is most beneficial to you and your heirs.

## Money-Boosting Strategies from Module 10:

Strategy #28: Protect and grow your income.
Strategy #29: Protect and grow your assets.
Strategy #30: Plan for the disbursement of your estate.
Strategy #31: Review your financial situation annually.

## Access these Module 10 exercises and resources at BrokeFreeForever.com:

Net Worth Calculation spreadsheet
Online home inventory Web site
Reflection Questions

# Module II:
## Rules of Engagement

*Character is what you are in the dark.*
—Dwight L. Moody

## ■ Shades of Grey

One of the most important and relevant areas of money management is the settlement of disputes. Most everything we do with money involves some kind of agreement with another, whether verbal, written, or implied. Many personal financial woes can be traced to a misunderstanding of the agreement, not understanding the implications or risk that you are agreeing to, or not knowing how best to stand up for yourself during a dispute.

There are many instances where people have lost money or paid more than they should have. It doesn't have to be like that. As the saying goes, the best defence is a good offence. Being offensive does not mean that you prepare to offend anyone; it means you have a plan for *approaching* a situation, as opposed to not being prepared and then being in a position where you need to *defend* yourself.

In sports and board games, you start with an understanding of the rules. In our society, we also have rules to guide us in our day-to-day interactions, from speed limits on the highway to filing a lawsuit in small claims court.

Rules can be made up by and vary from many different levels of rule makers: your parents' rules at home may differ from grandma's at her house. We are subject to rules made up by our employers, professional associations, unions, clubs and associations, and every level of government—municipal, provincial, state and federal.

Not all rules are black and white; our culture involves many areas of grey. Not all rules will fit every situation, and sometimes dispute resolution means interpreting the *intention* of a rule to fit a specific situation. You see, every law that has been created was done so with an *intention* to set boundaries or rules for all of us to get along in society. Unfortunately, the intention of any law and the *interpretation* (by a decision maker) are not always one and the same.

Frequently, the person with the *better understanding* of how to persuade a decision maker to adopt his or her interpretation of the facts is the one who wins the dispute. If you want to win your dispute, you'd best have a pretty persuasive argument as to why your opinion or position is the most logical (or reasonable) given all of the facts available.

Of course, on the flip side, many times, the person who has a valid argument for his or her point of view loses because he or she wasn't prepared or did not know how to properly prepare. He or she didn't have a good offence or a good defence.

⌘ ⌘ ⌘

### True Story: Crazed Christopher

Christopher was crazed with frustration! He had just talked to someone on the phone two weeks ago about his cell phone bill. He couldn't afford the $427 he owed, so he asked them to cancel his service until he could pay it off. Then he transferred $85 to this account through his online bill payments.

Today, he received a bill for over $800! What the !&*#@??

⌘ ⌘ ⌘

### *True Story: Moving Nancy*

Nancy was furious; that landlord of hers not only didn't give her her security deposit refund, she told Nancy she would put it in the mail in a couple of weeks!

Nancy was tired after just spending six hours cleaning out the apartment while her husband moved all their belongings to their new condo.

"Wait till Nick hears about this; he's going to freak out!" Nancy spewed to her friend as they packed the cleaning supplies into her car. "We really need that money; we were counting on it to help offset the cost of this move!" she cried as she threw the last cleaning bucket into the back seat.

⌘ ⌘ ⌘

In the examples above, both Christopher and Nancy are feeling that they have been done wrong by, and maybe they have. But before we can decide for ourselves, we need to remember that there are always at least two sides to a dispute (like or hate it; it's true!).

## ■ Six Rules for Engagement

*Note: The following information is intended as a personal opinion only and is not intended to be construed as legal advice. Always consult a lawyer, legal aid office, or other professional for advice concerning any contractual and legal issues you may be experiencing.*

### 1. Know the frame of reference.

Every dispute involves an actual or imagined breach of a promise or understanding between two people. To get to the heart of the matter, you need to understand the *frame of reference* of the dispute; that is, to which rules, understanding, contract, or obligation does the dispute refer?

Entering into an agreement, written or verbal, with someone is similar to creating and agreeing to your own rules for the activities you want to carry out. Think of a contract as an exchange of promises, but with the added security that breaking that promise can result in penalties or other discipline.

When a dispute arises while playing a board game, you turn to the rule sheet to determine how to proceed. In financial matters, there is always some form of reference that determines what the rules are, beginning with what form of agreement exists between the people (or businesses) involved and when necessary, what the relevant laws are. Usually, the individuals or businesses involved in a contract are referred to as the *parties*.

Because contracts are enforceable by the courts, it is essential that you know what you are getting into with every agreement that you make. That includes knowing your *obligations and responsibilities* for that cell phone service, renting that apartment or house, leasing that vehicle, and even accepting that job.

This means you need to read the contract and understand what every clause means. Consider every clause—what does the clause mean for you and how could it potentially be used against you? When you understand that, you will know the risk of every clause and whether you could live with the outcome if it were to be used against you. If you can live with the worst that could happen, you are prepared! If you don't understand what every clause in a contract means, then don't sign it until you do!

You can always ask for time to have someone review a contract with you. Ask a trusted friend, colleague, teacher, or a professional business person that you know if he or she would take a look at it and consider whether you should be getting some legal advice.

Minimum things you should consider before signing any contract:

* What are your obligations? What do you need to do, and when?
* What are the other party's obligations?
* What happens if you change your mind?

- ❀ What happens if you cannot continue to pay or fulfill your obligations?
- ❀ What are your options for ending the contract?
- ❀ When does it naturally end (terminate)?
- ❀ What is the worst thing that can happen for you, and can you live with that outcome?

## 2. Determine the issue(s) in dispute.

Once you have identified the rules you have to play within and the terms of the agreement between the parties, you need to identify specifically what *obligations or responsibilities* have been breached.

⌘ ⌘ ⌘

### *Back to Christopher*

Christopher dug through his files to find the contract that he signed at the store when he picked out his phone. That contract sets out the terms of payment, interest rates for overdue amounts, all fees he agreed to pay, and the termination fee that he is obligated to pay if he cancels his contract prior to the end of his term.

In Christopher's case, he signed a two-year term. Since he has only had the phone for six months, he still has eighteen months left on the contract. The termination fee he agreed to was $35 per month for all months remaining up to a maximum of $400 ($35 x 18 months = $630), so Christopher is actually getting the better end of the deal by having to pay *only* the maximum set penalty.

Now that the penalty to terminate the contract had been charged by the service provider, Christopher really understood just how expensive it was to cancel the contract he agreed to. He had signed up for a two-year service term so he wouldn't have to pay the $300 for his phone. It would have been cheaper for Christopher to buy his phone outright—and only agree to a month-by-month or pay-as-you-go contract.

⌘ ⌘ ⌘

## *Back to Nancy*

Two weeks later, Nancy received a cheque in the mail from her landlord. Instead of the $650 she had paid at the beginning of her tenancy term, the landlord returned only $276, claiming $354 in damages and cleaning charges.

Nancy was furious. "How dare she!" Nancy exclaimed to her husband. "That place was spotless when we left! I spent six hours cleaning! And she never said anything when she came down to inspect the apartment—if she had any concerns, she could have told me then!"

Nancy was going to call the landlord and demand the rest of the money. "Not so fast," Nick said, "there's a proper way to do this, and calling her might just make the situation worse." Nancy and Nick went to the residential tenancy website to determine their best course of action.

⌘ ⌘ ⌘

What, specifically, do you think are the issues that Nancy and Nick are disputing in this case?

In the province of British Columbia, a tenant must agree to the deductions made by the landlord, so the landlord did not have the right to withhold any portion of the security deposit paid by Nancy in the example above. Every situation can be different and include many relevant factors to be considered. Also, every jurisdiction has different rules, so it is very important to know the current laws of the province or state that you live in.

### 3. Understand the process you need to follow.

The rules that govern your dispute also include *how* to resolve your dispute. The rules might set out a place, a process, or a governing body (e.g., tribunal or arbitration board) that you must follow, together with any paperwork you must file, and how/where to file that paperwork.

The following is a clause from the back page of a monthly statement from a cellular service company (translation follows):

> 8. *Any claim, dispute or controversy (whether in contract or tort, pursuant to statute or regulation, or otherwise, and whether pre-existing, present or future) arising out of or relating to:*

a.  *this agreement;*

b. *the services or equipment provided to you by us;*

c. *oral or written statements, or advertisements or promotions relating to this agreement or to the services or equipment; or*

d. *the relationships which result from this agreement*

e. *(collectively the "Claim") will be determined by arbitration to the exclusion of the courts. You agree to waive any right you may have to commence or participate in any class action against us related to any Claim and, where applicable, you also agree to opt out of any class proceeding against us. Please give notices of any Claims to the address in Section 6. Arbitration will be conducted by one arbitrator pursuant to the laws and rules relating to commercial arbitration in the province in which you reside that are in effect on the date of the notice.*

**Translation** *(if you are a lawyer or a cellular service provider representative, please don't call me: the following is not intended to be taken literally—I'm just saying…):*

*No matter what your "Beef" is, whether it's already happened, is happening, or will happen, and whether it is related to anything we said, wrote, advertised, or included in a promotion, the said Beef **will be decided by an arbitrator and not by any court** (yes, you have waived your right to go to court), AND, you agree to not participate in any class action or proceeding against us (no matter what we've done or said, as above). Oh yes, and if you do have a claim, you must send it to us at the address in Section 6.*

Now, of course, you haven't actually agreed to these terms, *until you use your cell phone.* Using the service is typically an indication that you accept the terms set out in the agreement: acceptance by *conduct.*

In this case, if you did have a dispute, first, you'd need to notify the service provider by delivering your notice to the address specified (in Section 6)—regular mail will do unless it states otherwise, as will fax delivery if a fax number is provided.

An arbitrator would become involved if you and the service provider could not resolve the dispute yourselves. First, you would wait a reasonable amount of time for a response to the claim you submitted and try to resolve the dispute from there.

If you could not resolve the dispute (again, after a reasonable amount of time), then an arbitrator would become involved. What's missing in the example clause is who actually involves (requests the services) of the arbitrator, who decides who the arbitrator will be, and who will pay for it. Since all of the above is unstated, you can initiate the process by contacting an arbitrator or requesting the service provider to do so.

If you were Nancy or Nick, what steps would you need to take next to try to recover the rest of your security deposit? What do you think would happen in your province or state based on the information you find?

## 4. Assemble your evidence.

Now that you know what exactly you are disputing, what the rules are, and what the process is you need to follow, you need to start preparing your argument. To prepare a persuasive argument, you need to support your argument with evidence. Evidence is any proof you can muster up to help support your point of view.

*Evidence could include* (but is not limited to) receipts, letters, e-mail correspondences, employment records, contracts and other documents, cancelled cheques, invoices, credit card statements, tangible items, pictures, witnesses, etc. Typically, a third-party witness would present his or her version of events by filing an affidavit; that's a statement that is sworn in front of a lawyer or notary. Not all evidence is always admissible (useable), depending on the situation and the evidence. For example, in some jurisdictions you cannot record a conversation between two people without *both* parties giving their consent. Of course, if someone leaves a message in your voice mail, that could be fair game!

## Dear Diary

A frequently overlooked yet strong piece of evidence is a personal journal or calendar. It can be very important to keep track of confrontations, health matters, episodes of anxiety and distress, harassing statements or activities, or anything else that might form part of the evidence to prove how something has affected you.

This could be especially important after a physical accident, but I have seen it prove useful in the case of a landlord-tenant dispute as well. The landlord, whom I knew, was receiving harassing and threatening letters and calls from the disgruntled tenant. Over the period of a few months of keeping track, the landlord had enough evidence to justify a restraining order and an eviction notice for illegal behaviour.

I hope you will never need to keep track of such activities, but even when trying to resolve a customer support dispute, keep track of every telephone call and what was said.

### Just the Facts, Ma'am

It's easy to record the summary of a conversation once you get into the habit. Try writing every third or fourth word in a conversation, skipping the ones that don't add value to your notes like "the, it, she, you, he, said," etc. You can also leave out vowels to write a short form of a word: *phone call* becomes *phn cl*; *send letter request* becomes *snd ltr rqst*. You can still make out the general idea of the conversation later, and the more words you capture, the more accurate your notes will be.

Some notations I use are: TT (telephone call to), TF (telephone call from [name]), VM (voice-mail message left) and ML (message left with [name]). Of course, these would be followed by the date, a summary of the conversation, and what action items were to follow.

**Note:** Make sure you always record the name or employee/reference number of the person you speak with, and always make sure you get whatever was agreed to over the phone *in writing*. Ask the customer service representative to send an e-mail or a letter via Canada Post or the U.S. Postal Service (some companies prohibit e-mail communications). In the alternative, you summarize the understanding in writing and fax, mail or email it to the company. Just be sure to keep evidence of that communication; a registered post receipt, print a 'cc' copy of the email, or a transmission report from the facsimile.

### 5. Determine the offensive strategy.

In any sport or game of strategy, the defensive team would love to know the offensive plays! Knowing the strengths or weaknesses of the other party is important in resolving disputes too.

This is where the other side of the story comes in. No matter how much you believe your perspective to be the *right* one, the other party probably believes that theirs is too. To strengthen your own position, you need give some consideration to what the other party's position is.

* What issues do you think they will consider being the subject issues of the dispute?
* Will they interpret any clauses or terms differently?
* What facts or evidence will they be relying on in their argument?
* How will they respond to the facts and evidence that you present?

If you are having a difficult time trying to see the dispute from the other party's perspective, ask a friend to do so for you. A good role play will help you to prepare your position. But remember, the friend is doing you a favour by role-playing—don't take out your anger and frustration on him or her! The better your friend is at pretending to be the other party, the better prepared you will be when the time comes to defend your argument!

## 6. Know what remedies are available.

Just like when you have a cold, you may turn to ointments to make your nose feel better and vitamins to help speed the recovery. In a dispute, you also want to consider which remedies can fix the problem. Maybe you are seeking a reduction in costs or a refund of money paid; maybe you want an unsatisfactory product or service replaced. Depending on what the actual dispute is, there could be any number of potential remedies to solve the dispute and bring it to an end.

Remedies could include an *action* that has to be taken by one of the sides, a *financial* or *time* penalty, or even a *substitution* of a product or service. Essentially, what do you want to see happen to make things better? What is fair given the rules and obligations, and what actions or services have already been delivered?

In some cases, it may be possible to ask the deciding party for any costs of resolving the dispute to be paid. This sometimes can happen if one party has been unfair or the dispute caused unreasonable expense or penalty to one of the sides.

If you feel you have been unfairly taken advantage of or have a lot to lose, consider getting legal advice.

## Quick Facts

There are provincial and state laws that are designed to protect consumers when they purchase goods or services and provide the governing rules for many day-to-day transactions. Search online for provincial or state sale of goods and/or consumer protection information to learn more. See the Resources section for some links to help get you started.

## ■ He Said / She said!

We've all been there at some time. Typically, it's while trying to explain something to some stranger on the other end of the phone line in another country or an automated voice asking all the wrong questions.

Sometimes trying to get through to someone with warm blood in their veins on the other end of the phone line seems as likely as winning the lottery. It can be frustrating when you feel the need to talk to someone, *now*.

But throwing the phone doesn't work; neither does the stream of obscenities directed at the automated voice, or worse yet, at the human being you *do* finally get to talk to. Sure, you might feel a little bit better having relieved that rush of adrenaline, but your own blood pressure is up and the stress just may be killing you.

There are some secrets to getting someone to *help* you, not just pass you on to the next person, make a notation of "lunatic" on your customer record, or wield their own weight and limits of power by escalating your penalty cycle.

There are four phases to resolving a conflict:[53]

1. opening (approaching the other party),

2. identifying (describing the concern),

3. exploring (sharing information and perspectives and understanding motivations), and

4. closing (finding a solution agreeable to both parties)

Use the rules of engagement to help define your concern (identifying) and what solutions or remedies you are hoping to achieve (closing). Then, consider these tips in interpersonal relations to help you advance through the opening and exploring phases.

## Speak the right language.

Getting someone to understand your point of view is not always an easy task. There are all kinds of things that can interfere: emotions, personal perspectives and interpretations, and knowledge of the facts.

That's a lot of "noise" to get through when trying to explain something to someone! Because of all that noise, it is important to understand that not just any old language will do when trying to resolve a conflict.

The language that will help you to communicate your position clearly includes those terms you discovered while doing your research to determine the rules of engagement, including the *frame of reference* (rules, clauses), the *specific issues* (clauses and terms), and the *process* to be followed.

All of that is what you want to communicate; now you need to set yourself up for *how* to best communicate.

## Don't make it personal.

Referring to the other person's mother usually won't win you any friends and really doesn't have anything to do with the dispute anyway (unless she's the other party!).

Consider that the only perspective you can possibly represent is your own. That means you can communicate only from the perspective of "I," so use "I" statements to get your point across.

Start by identifying what the message is that you want to communicate. Write it down. Then, remove any references that include an emotion or an insult. For example, "Your company is a bunch of idiots that couldn't add two and two together if your life depended on it" does not communicate that there is an error in the addition on the invoice; instead, it communicates that you are angry and you are insulting the company the person on the phone works for.

Even if the person agrees, he or she probably isn't going to jump onto your side and try to help you; you just insulted the person and put him or her in a defensive position.

The key to having someone on the other end of the phone *hear and understand* your message is to clearly state your message in a non-personalized way and then ask that person how he or she can help you to resolve the issue.

*Download dispute resolution preparation worksheets from BrokeFreeForever.com.*

### Get past the gatekeeper.

Now that you have clearly and unemotionally communicated your message, you may find that the person you are speaking with does not have the power or influence to resolve the issue to your satisfaction. Even so, as the first person you must speak with, he or she is the gatekeeper. That means this is the person who can open the gate to help you move the process along or shut it fast and lock it if you are insulting or verbally abusive.

First, determine whom you are speaking with and what degree of influence he or she has to resolve your concern. Ask for his or her name or reference number and make a note of it. Then, communicate your request, concern, or points, and ask how he or she can help.

When talking to the gatekeepers, ask them: What are the limits of what they can do? Can they resolve this issue, or can they transfer your case to someone who can? What process do they need to follow before they can transfer you to an escalated process? Then help them move the process along by providing the necessary information and completing the necessary process.

### Create a paper trail.

Remember Hansel and Gretel and their bread-crumb trail? A paper trail is very similar. It is a trail of paper that someone could follow that sets out the information, dates, names, and steps that are related to resolving your concerns. Whether you put all the information in a binder, shoe box, envelope, file folder or a plastic bag doesn't matter; just make sure you keep it together somewhere for future reference.

Keep a written record of your phone conversations, including the date and name of the person you spoke with, and important points from the conversation. Sometimes it helps to write out some points *before* you are on the phone, and then you can just check off the points as you make them.

Keep these notes together with copies of any relevant invoices, letters, e-mails, receipts, warranty information, or any other information.

Keep this information in *chronological* order—organized by date; this makes it easier to review the process or steps taken and will help you to review the process when and if necessary. This paper trail can become a large part of your *evidence* if and when you need to settle a dispute.

# ■ Summary of Module 11

There are three guarantees in life: death, taxes, and the occasional interpersonal dispute! All conflict and dispute does not have to be ugly, however. Knowing how to best set yourself up for success is important, especially when it comes to financial matters. Module 11 sets out basic principles for representing yourself in a dispute situation and how to be proactive so you are ready should a dispute arise.

### Money-Boosting Strategies from Module 11:

Strategy #32: Understand your rights and your responsibilities.

Strategy #33: Be proactive for successful dispute resolution.

Strategy #34: Understand your own and others' communication capabilities.

Strategy #35: Use effective communication tools to aid in resolution.

### Access these Module 11 exercises and resources at BrokeFreeForever.com:

Dispute Resolution Preparation
Reflection Questions

# Resources

**Access these and additional links, tools and resources from Broke-FreeForever.com.**

Links disclaimer: These links were valid at the time of printing. Because these links are owned and updated by third parties, the publisher and author do not make any representations or accept any responsibility for the information contained within these sources. At the time of printing, the links were accurate and we considered the information worthwhile to include.

Send your recommendations for additional links to include to links@BrokeFreeForever.com

## Building Net Worth

Certified Financial Planner Board of Standards (U.S.)—Learn about Resources http://www.cfp.net/learn/clinic.asp
http://www.cfp.net/teamup/hr/links.asp

AICPA Personal Financial Planning Center
http://pfp.aicpa.org/Resources/

## Calculators

TMX Money Calculators
http://custom.marketwatch.com/custom/tsx/en/calculators/index.asp

Web Math Simple Interest Calculator
http://www.webmath.com/simpinterest.html

Young Money Calculators
http://www.youngmoney.com/calculators

MSN's Affordability Calculator
http://autos.msn.com/loancalc/newloan.aspx

Canada's Office of Consumer Affairs
http://www.ic.gc.ca/eic/site/oca-bc.nsf/eng/ca01812.html#result
http://canada.gc.ca/forms-formulaires/tools.html

Amortization Calculator
http://www.amortization-schedule.info/

Canada Mortgage and Housing—Total Debt Service Ratio Calculator
http://www.cmhc-schl.gc.ca/en/hoficlincl/moloin/molointo/molointo_005.cfm

BankRate.com Debt-Management Tools and Info
http://www.bankrate.com/calculators/index-of-debt-management-calculators.aspx
http://www.bankrate.com/calculators/managing-debt/loan-calculator.aspx

PayDay Loan calculator (Government of Alberta)
http://www.servicealberta.ca/1608.cfm

## Credit Counselling and Debt Management

The Public Interest Advocacy Centre (CDN)
http://www.piac.ca/information/

Consumers Council of Canada
http://www.consumerscouncil.com/

The Competition Bureau of Canada
http://www.competitionbureau.gc.ca/

Office of Consumer Affairs (CDN)
http://www.ic.gc.ca/eic/site/oca-bc.nsf/eng/home
*check out The Canadian Consumer Handbook*

Federal Trade Commission (USA) Bureau of Consumer Protection
http://www.ftc.gov/bcp/index.shtml

Consumer Federation of America
http://www.consumerfed.org/

Consumers Union
*Non-Profit Publisher of Consumer Reports*
http://www.consumersunion.org

National Consumers League
http://www.nclnet.org/

Canadian Association of Insolvency and Restructuring Professionals (CAIRP)
http://www.cairp.ca

Ontario Association of Credit Counselling Services (OACCS)
http://oaccs.ca

Canadian Association of Credit Counselling Services (CACCS)
http://caccs.ca

Credit Counselling Canada
http://www.creditcounsellingcanada.ca

Canadian Association of Independent Credit Counselling Agencies (CAICCA)
http://www.caicca.ca

Credit Counselling Canada Debt Quiz
http://www.creditcounsellingcanada.ca/ConsumerTools/Money-Quiz/tabid/78/Default.aspx

Association for Financial Counseling and Planning Education (AFCPE)
http://afcpe.org

National Foundation for Credit Counseling (NFCC)
http://nfcc.org

Association of Independent Consumer Credit Counseling Agencies (AICCCA)
www.aiccca.org

Dealing with Debt: A Consumer's Guide (Office of the Superintendent of Bankruptcy, Canada) http://www.ic.gc.ca/eic/site/bsf-osb.nsf/eng/br01861.html

BankRate.com Debt-Management Tools and Info
http://www.bankrate.com/debt-management.aspx

## Credit Reporting Agencies

Equifax
http://www.equifax.ca
http://www.equifax.com

TransUnion
http://www.transunion.ca
http://www.transunion.com

Annual Credit Report Service (US only)
www.annualcreditreport.com

## General Learning and Financial Industry

Consumer Protection Resources and Information
http://www.bpcpa.ca/

Financial Consumer Agency of Canada
http://www.fcac-acfc.gc.ca/eng/default.asp

Young Money
http://www.youngmoney.com/

Canadian Payday Loan Association
http://www.cpla-acps.ca

Consumer Federation of America
http://www.consumerfed.org/

Consumer Federation of America Payday Loan Consumer Information
http://www.paydayloaninfo.org/default.asp

Canada's Office of Consumer Affairs |Money, Credit & Debt
http://www.ic.gc.ca/eic/site/oca-bc.nsf/eng/h_ca02222.html

Canada's Office of Consumer Affairs | Credit, Loans & Debt
http://www.fcac-acfc.gc.ca/eng/consumers/CreditLoanDebt/default.asp

## Getting to Know Yourself

| | |
|---|---|
| Personality assessments | www.2h.com/personality-tests.html |
| Psychology Today | http://www.psychologytoday.com/tests/ |
| Keirsey Instrument | http://www.keirsey.com/sorter/instruments2.aspx?partid=0 |
| Locus of Control | http://www.psych.uncc.edu/pagoolka/LocusofControl-intro.html |

# Notes

1    E. Torry Higgins, "Beyond Pleasure and Pain," *American Psychologist* 52 (December), 1280–1300.

2    Jordi Quoidback, Elizabeth W. Dunn, K. V. Petrides, and Moira Mikolajczak, "Money Giveth, Money Taketh Away: The Dual Effect of Wealth on Happiness," *Psychological Science* (in press).

3    Walter Mischel, *Personality and Assessment* (New York: John Wiley, 1968).

4    J. Metcalfe and W. Mishel, "A Hot/Cool-System Analysis of Delay of Gratification: Dynamics of Willpower," *Psychological Review* (1999): 3–19.

5    Baumeister, "Yielding to Temptation: Self-Control Failure, Impulsive Purchasing, and Consumer Behavior," *Journal of Consumer Research* (2002): 670–676.

6    L. Michael Hall, PhD, "The Magical Nature of Beliefs," *The International Society of Neuro-Semantics* (2007), http://www.neurose-mantics.com (accessed January 2010).

7    J. B. Rotter, C. L. Cooper, and J. I. Sanchez, "Locus of Control and Well-Being at Work: How Generalizable Are Western Findings?" *Academy of Management Journal* (2002): 453–456.

8    B. M. Bass, *Bass & Stogdill's Handbook of Leadership,* 34th ed. (New York: Free Press, 1990).

9    Derek D. Rucker and Adam D. Galinsky, "Desire to Acquire: Powerlessness and Compensatory Consumption," *Journal of Consumer Research* (2008): 257–267.

10    Timbuk 3, "The Future's So Bright, I Gotta Wear Shades" [perf.], Timbuk3, [comps.], Pat MacDonald, *Greetings from Timbuk 3*, s.l.: I.R.S. Records (1986).

11    Gary Chapman, *The Five Love Languages* (Chicago: Northfield Publishing, 2004).

12    A. H. Maslow. *Motivation and Personality* (New York: Harper and Row, 1954).

13    Baumeister, "Yielding to Temptation: Self-Control Failure, Impulsive Purchasing, and Consumer Behavior," *Journal of Consumer Research* (2002): 670–676.

14    Loran Nordgren, Joop van der Pligt, and Frank van Harreveld, "The Restraint Bias: How the Illusion of Self-Restraint Promotes Impulsive Behavior," *Psychological Science* (2009): 1523–1528.

15    J. M. Digman, "Personality Structure: Emergence of the Five-Factor model," *Annual Review of Psychology* 41 (1990) 417–440, as cited in Stephen P. Robbins and Nancy Langton, *Fundamentals of Organizational Behaviour*. 2nd ed. (Toronto, ON: Pearson Prentice Hall, 2004).

16    R. Catell, "Personality Pinned Down," *Psychology Today* , (1973): 40-46

17    W. G Huitt, "Problem Solving and Decision Making: Consideration of Individual Differences Using the Myers-Briggs Type Indicator," *Journal of Psychological Type*, 24, (33–44), as cited in Judy McKenna, Karen Hyllegard, and Ray Linder, "Linking Psychological Type to Financial Decision-Making," *Financial Counseling and Planning* 14, no. 1 (2003).

18    G. W. Allport and H. S. Odbert, "Traitnames. A Psycho-lexical Study," *Psychological Monographs* (1936): 171.

19    G. Scott Acton, "Five-Factor Model," *Great Ideas in Personality*, http://www.personalityresearch.org/bigfive.html (accessed May 25, 2010).

20    Kathleen Gurney, PhD, *Your Money Personality: What It Is and How You Can Profit from It*, Financial Psychology Corporation (2009).

21    Sandy L. Aaker and Angela Y. Lee, "'I' Seek Pleasures and 'We' Avoid Pains: The Role of Self-Regulatory Goals in Information Pro-

cessing and Persuasion," *Journal of Consumer Research* 28 (2001): 33–49.

22   Scott I. Rick, Cynthia E. Cryder, and George Loewenstein, "Tightwads and Spendthrifts," *Journal of Consumer Research* 34 (2008): 767–782.

23   John L. Lastovicka, "Lifestyle of the Tight and Frugal: Theory and Measurement," *Journal of Consumer Research* (1999).

24   Barret Strong, "Money That's What I Want," *Money (That's What I Want)*, by Barry Gordy Jr. and Janie Bradford, Motown Records (1959).

25   Annamaria Lusardi and Peter Tufano, "Teach Workers about the Perils of Debt," *Harvard Business Review*, November (2009): 22.

26   Certified General Accountants Association of Canada. *Where Has the Money Gone: The State of Canadian Household Debt in a Stumbling Economy*, www.cga.org/canada (accessed October, 2009).

27   Andrew Kitching and Sheena Starky, *Parliament of Canada*, 28 September 2007, http://www2.parl.gc.ca/Sites/LOP/LegislativeSummaries (accessed October, 2009).

28   Ruth E Berry and Karen A. Duncan, "The Importance of Payday Loans in Canadian Consumer Insolvency," 31 October 2007, http://www.ic.gc.ca/eic/site/bsf-osb.nsf/eng/br02026.html (accessed October, 2009).

29   Canadian Payday Loan Association. Press Releases (2009), http://www.cpla-acps.ca/english/mediareleases.php (accessed September, 2009).

30   Payday Loan Consumer Information, Consumer Federation of America, http://www.paydayloaninfo.org/legal.asp (accessed September, 2009).

31   Canadian Payday Loan Association, "Code of Conduct," October 2009, http://www.cpla-acps.ca/english/consumercode.php (accessed September, 2009).

32   Canadian Bankers Association, "The Banking Industry in Canada" (2006).

33   Ibid.

34   "Canadian Workers Living from Paycheque to Paycheque: Employees Worried about the Economy, Debt and Retirement," Canadian Payroll Association press release (Toronto, ON: September 13, 2010).

35    "Majority of Canadian employees living paycheque to pay-cheque, not saving enough for retirement. Younger workers and single parents having most trouble making ends meet," Canadian Payroll Association press release (Toronto, ON: September 14, 2009).

36    Gulden Ulkumen, Manoj Thomas, and Vicki Morwitz, "Will I Spend More in 12 Months or a Year?" *Journal of Consumer Research* (2008): 245–256.

37    Derek D. Rucker and Adam D. Galinsky, "Desire to Acquire: Powerlessness and Compensatory Consumption," *Journal of Consumer Research* (2008): 257–267.

38    Baumeister, "Yielding to Temptation: Self-Control Failure, Impulsive Purchasing, and Consumer Behavior," *Journal of Consumer Research* (2002): 670–676.

39    Statistics Canada, *Survey of Household Spending, 2006*, 26 February 2008.

40    Statistics Canada, *Changing Patterns in Canadian Homeownership and Shelter Costs, 2006, Census: Comparing Shelter Costs to Income*, Ottawa: 4 June 2008.

41    Statistics Canada, *Median Total Income, by Family Type, by Province and Territory*, CANSIM table 111-0009, 2006.

42    Statistics Canada, *Survey of Household Spending, 2006*, 26 February 2008.

43    U.S. Census Bureau, Current Population Reports, Series P60-235. Table 676, *Money Income of Households—Distribution by Income Level and Selected Characteristics* 2007.

44    U.S. Bureau of Labor Statistics, Consumer Expenditures in 2007. News, USDL-08-1746 (published 25 November 2008) and earlier reports, Table 671, *Average Annual Expenditures of All Consumer Units by Region and Size of Unit* 2007.

45    Credit Counselling Society, "Information Articles," *Credit Counselling Society*, December 2008, http://www.nomoredebts.org/articles.shtml (accessed February, 2010).

46    Shubhasis Dey, Ramdane Djoudad, and Yaz Terajima, Department of Monetary and Financial Analysis, "A Tool for Assessing Financial Vulnerabilities in the Household Sector," *Bank of Canada Review*, Summer 2008.

47    The Federal Reserve Board, "Household Debt Service and Financial Obligations Ratios," December 17, 2010, http://www.federalreserve.gov/releases/housedebt (accessed September, 2009).

48    William Bridges, *Managing Transitions, Making the Most of Change* (Cambridge: Da Capo Press, 2003).

49    Larry Hershfield, Shawn Chirrey, Jodi Thesenvitz, and Urmila Chandran, "Changing Behaviours: A Practical Framework," *The Health Communication Unit* (2004), http://www.thcu.ca (accessed January 2010).

50    Thomas J. Stanley and William D. Danko, *The Millionaire Next Door* (Marietta: Pocket Books, 1996).

51    Sir John Templeton, "Franklin Templeton Investments Investor Resource Center," *Franklin Templeton Investments*, https://www.franklintempleton.com (accessed January 2010).

52    *Insurance Hotline*, November 2009, http://www.insurancehotline.com, (accessed November 2009).

53    Justice Institute of British Columbia. *Conflict Resolution* (13th ed.) (2005). New Westminster: Justice Institute of British Columbia, Centre for Conflict Resolution.

# About the author

Pamela Nelson, MBA, has been helping individuals improve their personal money management habits for years as a business advisor, loans analyst and coach. As a single-mom and sole provider for her own household Pamela learned to dig herself out from under massive debt and keep more money from each payday, overcoming her own financial struggles through proactive and cost-cutting strategies. While earning her master's degree in business, Pamela took a special interest in consumer behavior: the behavior related to spending money. In *Broke-Free Forever* Pamela melds her practical approach and real-life experience with principles of business financial management and consumer behavior, culminating in strategies to help anyone who wants to stop being broke, and break the cycle of living payday-to-payday, for good.

Made in the USA
Charleston, SC
31 July 2011